MOLIÈRE

WORLD DRAMATISTS

OLIÈRE

GERTRUD MANDER

Translated by Diana Stone Peters

WITH HALFTONE ILLUSTRATIONS

FREDERICK UNGAR PUBLISHING CO.
NEW YORK

Published by arrangement with Friedrich Verlag,
Velber, Germany

Copyright © 1973 by Frederick Ungar Publishing Co., Inc.
Printed in the United States of America
Library of Congress Catalog Card Number: 70-163147
Designed by Edith Fowler
ISBN: 0-8044-2662-7 (cloth)

CONTENTS

1748228

CHRONOLOGY

1621   In the parish of Saint-Eustache, Jean Poquelin, the son and grandson of master upholsterers, marries Marie Cressé, the daughter
and granddaughter of master upholsterers.

1622   January 15th. Jean-Baptiste Poquelin, the
eldest of six children of whom only four survive, is baptized in the church of Saint-
Eustache. Malherbe and his contemporaries
—the founders of French classicism—are
dead. Corneille is a student in Rome. Tragedies are performed at the universities.

1631   Jean Poquelin buys the office of *tapissier
ordinaire du Roi* (upholsterer-in-ordinary to
the King) from his brother. This office carries with it the honorary title of Squire and
an annuity. The dramatist Hardy, who has
written more than one hundred plays, dies.
Corneille makes his debut with *Mélite*, a
comedy.

1632   After the death of Marie Cressé, Jean Poque-
        lin remarries and rents a house near Les
        Halles. Jean-Baptiste grows up in the live-
        liest quarter of Paris, between Les Halles,
        the Hôtel de Rambouillet and the Pont
        Neuf. Like nearly all of the great writers of
        his day, he is educated by the Jesuits of the
        College of Clermont. His friends there are
        Bernier, the great world traveler; Chapelle,
        the drunkard; and Cyrano de Bergerac, all
        of whom are future *libertins*, or freethink-
        ers. His maternal grandfather often takes
        him along to the Hôtel de Bourgogne to
        see the tragedies of the *Grands Comédiens*
        and the farces of the *Comédiens Italiens*.

1636   Corneille becomes famous as a result of the
        conflict surrounding *Le Cid*. The young
        Poquelin takes the oath of succession as
        tapissier du Roi. Upon completion of his
        secondary-school education, he begins to
        study law and prepare for the office of
        notary.

1638   Louis XIV is born. Descartes's *Discours de la
        Methode* (Discourse on Method) appears.

1640   Tibrio Fiorelli, known as Scaramouche, ar-
        rives in Paris. (He was to free the Italian
        comedy from its verbal tradition by employ-
        ing pantomime as his chief form of expres-
        sion.) Jean-Baptiste Poquelin becomes ac-
        quainted with Scaramouche and possibly
        takes lessons from him. At this time he also
        meets Madeleine Béjart, a twenty-two-year-

old actress and the daughter of a court official.

1641 Jean-Baptiste Poquelin is confirmed as a notary. In order to keep him away from Madeleine, Jean-Baptiste's father sends him in his own place with the court when it moves to Narbonne. However, he meets Madeleine once again in Narbonne.

1642 Richelieu and Louis XIII die. Descartes's *Meditations* appears.

1643 Jean-Baptiste Poquelin decides to go into the theater. On January 6th, he renounces the right of succession to his father's court appointment. Although he is not yet of age, he is allowed to have his own way, but his father withdraws financial support.

In February, Madeleine gives birth to a daughter who is christened Armande and later known as Menou.

On June 30th, Jean-Baptiste Poquelin, together with Madeleine Béjart, her brother Joseph, Geneviève Béjart, and nine other actors, signs the contract establishing the Illustre Théâtre. Only Madeleine Béjart has the right "to select those roles for herself which she wishes to play." Jean-Baptiste shares the tragic roles with two other actors. On September 12th, the Illustre Théâtre rents the Gardeners' Tennis Courts near the gate of Nesles, now called Rue Mazarine.

1644   On January 1st, the Illustre Théâtre opens.
        It has two rivals: the Hôtel de Bourgogne
        and the Théâtre du Marais. Plays by Cor-
        neille and du Ryer are performed without
        much success. Tristan l'Hermite finances the
        troupe which is now managed by Jean-
        Baptiste Poquelin under the name of Molière.
        The Illustre Théâtre accumulates debts,
        loses a series of actors, gives up its original
        premises, and moves to the Croix Noire
        (Quai des Celestins).

        The candle dealer Antoine Faussier has
        Molière imprisoned in the Châtelet for two
        unpaid bills. The good-natured pavior Leon-
        ard Aubry posts the required bail for his re-
        lease. Molière's father rescues him from this
        affair by repaying Aubry's loan. The Illustre
        Théâtre disbands.

1645   At the end of the year, Molière, Joseph,
        Madeleine, and Geneviève Béjart join the
        Dufresne troupe to which René Berthelot,
        known by the names of Du Parc and Gros-
        René, already belongs. This troupe numbers
        about twenty to twenty-five actors. A period
        of touring now begins which will last until
        1658. According to contemporary reports,
        there were some twelve to fifteen similar
        groups of itinerant players performing
        throughout France. The troupe which
        Molière has joined enjoys the patronage of
        the Duc d'Éperon.

1650–51 Molière has advanced to the position of the
        troupe's Principal. He becomes the favorite

actor of the Prince de Conti who grants the troupe a pension.

1654   In Lyon, Molière encounters the Italian Comedians.

He writes his first scenarios and his first play, *L'Etourdi* (The Blunderer). After a religious conversion, the Prince de Conti withdraws his patronage and becomes Molière's most bitter opponent in the Society of the Holy Sacrament.

1656–57 The troupe performs in the southwest of France and in the region of Lyon-Dijon.

1658   The troupe moves to Rouen and prepares for its return to Paris. In Rouen they perform in the Braques Tennis Courts. Corneille writes his amorous rhymes to the "Marquise" Du Parc, the wife of Gros-René and a leading lady in Molière's troupe.

On October 24th, the troupe plays before the King in the Louvre. The King is somewhat bored by Corneille's *Nicomède* but enjoys Molière's farce *Le Docteur amoureux* (The Doctor in Love). This is the troupe's great chance. The King's brother, known as "Monsieur," takes over the patronage of the actors. On November 2nd, they move into the Théâtre du Petit-Bourbon, which they share with the Italian Comedians. The Italians perform on *jours ordinaires* (regular days) or Sundays, Mondays, and Wednesdays. Molière must be content with the remaining days.

1659   After July 7th, when the Italians return to Italy, the Petit-Bourbon belongs entirely to Molière's troupe. The old plays of Corneille are performed without much success. Molière has no success with tragedy. He decides to revive his own plays *The Blunderer* and *Le Dépit amoureux* (The Amorous Quarrel), which win him the immediate favor of the King. The triumph of *Les Précieuses ridicules* (The Precious Damsels) on November 18th antagonizes Molière's rivals at the Hôtel de Bourgogne.

1660   Mazarin dies. Louis XIV marries. Boileau's first satire appears. Goaded on by Molière's rivals, Monsieur de Ratabon, the Royal Surveyor, has the Petit-Bourbon torn down in order to enlarge the Louvre. Molière now has no theater and the troupe remains unemployed for three months. But the actors remain loyal to Molière. The King places the great hall of the Palais Royal at his disposal. However, this hall is small and poorly fitted out. Its ceiling consists of a blue cloth held in place by cords. The troupe performs *Sganarelle, ou Le Cocu imaginaire* (Sganarelle, or the Imaginary Cuckold). As a cautionary measure, Molière once again assumes the rights of succession to the court office of his father, with whom he has become reconciled.

1661   Final return of the Italians, accompanied by
        Domenico Biancolelli, the great Harlequin.
        Domenico becomes Molière's friend. The
        failure of *Dom Garcie de Navarre* (Don
        Garcia of Navarre) is balanced by the suc-
        cess of *L'École des maris* (The School for
        Husbands) and of *Les Fâcheux* (The Bores).
        Molière rents a house behind the Palais
        Royal in the Rue Saint-Thomas du Louvre.
        Construction begins on the enlargement of
        Versailles.

1662   On January 23rd, the marriage contract be-
        tween the forty-year-old Molière and Ar-
        mande Béjart, who is "approximately twenty
        years old," is signed. The bride is the sister
        —some say the daughter—of Madeleine
        Béjart. On December 26th, Molière performs
        L'École des femmes (The School for
        Wives).

1663   Pascal dies. The conflict over *The School
        for Wives* marks the beginning of Molière's
        difficulties. On January 1st, Boileau writes
        verses directed against the opponents of *The
        School for Wives*. On March 17th, the play
        is published with a preface by Molière. An
        attempt is made to have the play suppressed.
        On June 1st, *La Critique de L'École des
        femmes* (The Critique of the School for
        Wives) appears. In August, *Zélinde, ou La
        Veritable Critique de l'école* (Celinde, or the
        True Critique of the School) appears in
        which Donneau de Visé charges Molière
        with godlessness.

In October, Boursault stages the *Portrait of the Painter* in which Molière is portrayed as a cuckold. Molière attends a performance at the Hôtel de Bourgogne. Urged on by Louis XIV, Molière performs *The Versailles Impromptu* for the King on the 18th or 19th of October. The *Impromptu* then appears on the Paris stage on November 4th. In the weeks to follow, Molière's opponents respond with *The Marquis's Revenge* by Donneau de Visé and with *The Improvisations of the Hôtel de Condé* by Montfleury (the son of the famous actor of the Hôtel de Bourgogne), who more or less openly accuses Molière of incest.

1664   On January 10th a son is born to Molière. Louis XIV acts as godfather. The child dies in November. In May, the great festival performance *Les Plaisirs de l'Île Enchanté* (The Pleasures of the Enchanted Isle) takes place at Versailles. The King had commissioned this work for his mistress Mademoiselle de La Vallière under the pretext of wishing to honor the Queen. Molière's troupe takes part in the processions and ensembles. On May 8th, *La Princesses d'Élide* (The Princess of Elis) is performed.

On May 12th, Molière performs the first three acts of *Tartuffe* for the King. The *Tartuffe* affair begins at this point. Even before the play has been completed, the Society of the Holy Sacrament undertakes action and with the support of the Queen

Mother obtains an interdiction against its performance. The Curé Roullé characterizes Molière as a "man, or rather a demon incarnate dressed in man's clothing, the most godless and irreligious man who has ever existed," and condemns him to the "flames of hell."

Molière has his play formally approved by the legate Chili and submits his first petition to the King. It meets with no success. He performs and reads *Tartuffe* only before friends and invited guests, but he goes on to complete it.

Boileau dedicates his second satire to Molière. Molière performs *La Thébaïde* (The Theban Brothers), Racine's first play.

1665   Molière quarrels with Racine over the latter's *Alexandre*. *Tartuffe* remains under interdiction. The repertoire is taken up once again. At the behest of his actors, Molière writes *Don Juan* which is performed on February 15th and is played with great success until the end of the theater season on March 20th. By the beginning of the next season—only three weeks later—*Don Juan* has disappeared from the billboards. There was no formal prohibition, but discreet pressure was put upon Molière to withdraw his play. The "Observations sur la Comédie de Don Juan" (Observations on the Comedy Don Juan) appear; this anti-Molière pamphlet is thought to be the work of a member of the Port-Royal circle. On September 15th Molière,

who is now having difficulties with his land-
lord, the well-known Doctor Daquin, stages
L'Amour médecin (Love's the Best Doctor).
Louis XIV takes over the patronage of
Molière's troupe and grants him a pension.

1666   The *Tartuffe* affair drags on. A daughter,
Ésprit-Madeleine, is born to Molière; Madeleine Béjart and the Duke de Modene stand
as godparents. Molière is sick and cannot act
for three months. At about the same time,
his difficulties with Armande begin.

Boileau tries in vain to persuade Molière to
give up the theater. He rents a county house
in Anteuil. On June 4th, Moliere's troupe
performs *Le Misanthrope* (The Misanthrope), on which he has worked for two
years. This masterpiece enjoys uncertain
success until it is performed together with
Le Médecin malgré lui (The Doctor in
Spite of Himself).

1667   The King joins his army in Flanders. Molière, believing himself to be in possession of
royal authorization, performs *L'Imposteur*
(The Impostor), a milder version of *Tartuffe*. The next day President de Lamoignon
forbids the performance. The Archbishop
Hardouin de Péréfixe enters the conflict
shortly thereafter. Boileau and Molière call
on Lamoignon who, like Tartuffe, dismisses
them with the excuse that he has to go to
mass. The two musketeers of the troupe, La

Grange and La Thorillère, go to the King with a second—unsuccessful—petition.

1668   La Fontaine publishes his first book of *Fables*. Mignard, one of Molière's best friends and his portraitist, dies.

On January 13th, Molière stages *Amphitryon* at the Palais Royal. In July, *Georges Dandin* appears with moderate success. On September 9th, *L'Avare* (The Miser) appears and proves to be a fiasco. Molière is very ill. He now lives apart from Armande, whom he only sees on the stage. Molière lends money to his father whose business has declined.

1670   On February 5th, permission is granted for *Tartuffe* to be performed. That very evening a crowd rushes to the box office and the play remains on the schedule until Easter. The play is published with a long preface by Molière. Molière's father, having been reduced to near total poverty, dies on February 25th. Molière produces mostly ballet-comedy: *Les Amants magnifiques* (The Magnificent Lovers), *Monsieur de Pourceaugnac*, and *Le Bourgeois gentilhomme* (The Would-Be Gentleman). The last of these three plays is a great success.

1671   In preparation for his production of *Psyché*, Molière has the hall at the Palais Royal renovated. Versailles becomes the seat of court. Molière performs *Les Fourberies de Scapin*

(The Mischievous Machinations of Scapin) and *La Comtesse d'Escarbagnas* (The Countess of Escarbagnas). He also writes *Les Femmes savantes* (The Learned Women).

1672   Molière is fifty years old. His second son, Pierre, is born but, like the first boy, does not survive. Molière quarrels with Lully, who has intrigued against him in order to obtain for his Académie Royale the sole privilege of staging all ballet and music festivals.

1673   Molière's last play, *Le Malade imaginaire* (The Imaginary Invalid), with music by Charpentier is not performed at court because Lully has intrigued against him once again. Molière loses the King's favor at precisely that moment when his physical powers also desert him.

On February 17th, during the fourth performance of *The Imaginary Invalid*, Molière has an attack on the stage and is carried to his home on the Rue de Richelieu. His request to see a priest is not granted, and he dies during the night. The curé of Saint-Eustache forbids his interment in consecrated ground. The actor Baron and then Armande call upon the King, who advises the Archbishop to avoid a scandal.

On February 21st, Molière is buried during the night in the cemetery of Saint-Joseph. Lully takes over the Palais Royal in order to convert it into an opera house. La Grange and Armande transplant the troupe to the

Rue Guénégaud, where they form an association with the actors of the Théâtre du Marais.

1674   Rumors circulate that Molière's corpse has been exhumed and thrown into the mass grave for unbaptized persons.

1680   The King joins the troupe from the Rue Guénégaud to that of the Hôtel de Bourgogne, thus establishing the Comédie Française.

1792   The alleged remains of Molière and La Fontaine are exhumed and brought to the Cloister of the Petit-Augustins. In 1817, they are transferred to the cemetery of Père Lachaise.

MOLIÈRE'S AGE
AND ACHIEVEMENT

"Molière," said Goethe, "is so great that we are always newly astonished whenever we read him. He is a man apart. His plays border on the tragic. They show intuitive understanding, and no one is intrepid enough to equal his accomplishment. I read a few of Molière's plays every year . . . for we small men are not able to preserve the greatness of such things within us. . . ."

Goethe's admirable appraisal of the classical French dramatist has never been contested. Over the centuries, critics, authors, actors, and audiences have echoed Goethe's opinion in a thousand variations. From his own time to the present, Molière has been considered the greatest comic dramatist in the history of European theater—a star of Shakespeare's magnitude beside whom dramatists from other ages and countries pale. We stand in awe before such greatness. As Goethe wrote: "We small men are not able to preserve the greatness of such things within us. . . ." I would like to add to this statement the verb "to describe," since I feel dwarfed by Molière's *oeuvre* and the enormous body of scholarly secondary literature it has produced. Though the latter offers various hypotheses and contradictory interpretations, there is one common denominator among all of this critical material: Molière is indeed unsurpassed. He is, like Shakespeare, a man "for all time." His plays have remained fresh and lively, having managed to survive a period of three hundred years in which each age offered new interpretations reflecting its own prevailing spirit. There is no reason to doubt that these plays will continue to remain fresh indefinitely.

There was no doubt about Molière's greatness practically from the beginning of his career. Even in the 1660s and 1670s the bourgeois Jean-Baptiste Poquelin who, under the stage name of Molière, was known to the Parisian theatergoers and members of Louis XIV's court as a director, a comic actor, and as a writer of farces, comedies, and plays for court festivals, was considered to be "France's foremost actor of farce" and the "King of Laughter." As both an actor and a writer, he really had no rivals. At most, he had opponents whose number grew as he became ever more successful.

The historical aspect of critical judgments concerning Molière as a writer is significant. Goethe was the first to assess his greatness as a playwright in terms of a comic talent that bordered on the tragic. However, it was above all Molière's ability to make them laugh heartily and happily that his contemporaries praised as being great and unsurpassable. As soon as Molière's declared primary purpose of entertaining his audience (*plaire*) became adulterated with other purposes—or so the public thought—the great majority of his contemporaries became disaffected and stayed away. This public found disturbing precisely that quality which we today consider the hallmark of his really great comedies.

It is significant that Goethe, a man of another age, speaks of reading Molière's plays and refers above all to those dramas (particularly *The Miser*) which triumphed on the stage only after their author's death. The Frenchman of the late seventeenth century was, however, blind to the literary value of these works. For him, Molière was not an author to be read like the great tragedians or the contemporary comic writers whose works were derived solely from the tradition of classical comedy. Molière's art had grown up on the boards, and thus its origins were in the daily practice of acting and in Molière's observation of popular or folk comedians who specialized in improvisation. It was to be sought (and found) on the stage. It was not literature as such, composed at a desk and then mounted for the theater; rather, it was virtually conceived on the spot where it was to be played, arising *from* the medium of the theater *for* the medium of the theater.

Stages of all varieties conditioned Molière's viewpoint and perspective: first, the traveling theater in the provinces, then his own theater in Paris and the outdoor theaters in Versailles, Vaux, etc.—erected as and when they were needed—and finally, those rooms in the palaces of the King or the high aristocracy, at

court or elsewhere, which were transformed into a
theater for a particular performance. Molière's function was a social one, and he himself understood it as
such. He wanted to entertain, always more and always
better.

Whom did he wish to entertain? A very heterogeneous, very spoiled, and generally well-educated public (at least after Molière had established himself in
Paris): the middle and upper-middle classes of the
city, the aristocrats and officials at court, the royal
family and, last but not least, the head of the state, the
Sun King himself, who was obsessed with the theater.
This meant that Molière had to have a particular instinct for his craft, for the spirit of the age, and for
the needs of such a demanding public. To function
effectively in this way, an author cannot remain
within his subjective world; by creating solely from
within himself those things suggested by obscure creative impulses, he consumes all of his energy in the
presentation of his own ideas, of his own view of the
world, of his own specific experiences of life, forgetting or disregarding his age and his readers.

Molière's creative process, however, was determined to the highest degree by the events taking place
all around him, by practical factors pertaining to his
specific craft, by economic considerations, and by the
financial dependence of others. He had to be successful because he was not only responsible for himself,
but for a whole troupe which depended upon him.
These actors needed both a livelihood and new roles,
and they performed nearly every day. The man,
whom later generations honor as preeminent among

writers of comedy, whom they understand primarily
through the texts of his plays, was known to his contemporaries in other capacities as well. Above all they
knew him as an excellent actor who wrote roles and
plays not only in character with his own nimble figure, his effervescent manner, and his tricks of mimicry, but also in keeping with the abilities of the other
players in his troupe.

Our age has rediscovered something about Molière
which his own age knew and treasured in him;
namely, that he was not a *littérateur* whose art was
primarily concerned with words. Nor was he a moralist who used the theater as a tool for some nontheatri-
cal end. They knew—and we learned—that from head
to toe he was a man of the theater who never wrote a
single word that was not conceived of as being either
spoken on a stage or translatable into mime, no scene
which could not be rounded off into a theatrical
whole, and no play which could achieve its ultimate
effectiveness without being performed on a stage.

Because of this, he could give to his age everything
it most ardently desired. For this was an age seized
with a true passion for the theater, for which the stage
meant the world, dream meant life, and art meant the
highest form of truth. But this age erred in one way:
with few exceptions, among whom—fortunately—was
the King himself, theatergoers accepted Molière's genius only up to a certain point. Because they wanted
only ready pleasure, blunt jests, fantasy, and cheerfulness, but not the finesse or edge of satire, nor anything
requiring thoughtfulness, they failed to value in Molière precisely what seemed greatest to later genera-

tions. Molière's contemporaries failed to appreciate *Tartuffe*, *Don Juan*, *The School for Wives*, *The Misanthrope* and *The Miser*, the very plays upon which he worked longest and most carefully and into which he poured his greatest knowledge of human beings and his greatest criticism of humanity. All the great comedies of character which provide entertainment on a deeper level have fared better with later generations than with Molière's contemporaries, who wanted only grotesque farce, mythological fantasies, pure theater free of moral and message—in other words, as much illusion and as little reality as possible.

In the middle of his Parisian career, Molière apparently underwent a change of heart. Turning from the maxim that it is prudent to adapt oneself to society, as argued in many of his plays, he produced in succession three plays—*Tartuffe*, *Don Juan* and *The Misanthrope* —that incurred the public's displeasure and invited actual suppression. But after the bitterness and near tragedy associated with *The Misanthrope*, which raised considerable doubts about the possibility of behaving honestly and genuinely in a corrupt society, he returned to a cheerful acceptance of his environment and set limits to his humorous criticism. In the future he avoided themes which touched too heavily upon the sore spots of his contemporaries or which challenged their overall view of the world and society. As in his earlier plays, Molière directed his criticism only toward individual social types and social phenomena, and so he was restored to his public's full favor.

Did society triumph and destroy something essential and fundamentally rebellious in Molière? Or did per-

sonal experience lead him to adopt a cheerful and conciliatory spirit so that in future he would be attacked
only for particular details in his work rather than for
larger concepts? Was he more concerned with professional advancement than with fundamental ideas? Did
he realize that he had reached the limits of comedy
and that beyond lay a no man's land into which very
few were ready to follow him (not even his royal
protector, who had rescued *Tartuffe* only after long
hesitation and resistance)?

Scholars are still trying to solve this riddle. Lacking
direct autobiographical evidence and basing our judgments on the texts themselves, on the history of their
performances, and on assorted polemical material for
and against Molière, we can only surmise that his theater, the practice of his art, and the favor of both the
public and the King were life-necessities for him. It is
perhaps also possible that as with Shakespeare the
cheerfulness of his art enabled him to surmount a grim
personal period filled with extreme doubts and despair.
For although the difficulties of his private life increased (e.g., his "incompatible" marriage, illness, conflict with his rival Lully, the intrigues of certain parties both at court and in the city), his artistic vitality,
his sense of the comic, and his poetic imagination were
not adversely affected. And it is precisely this adaptability, which permitted Molière seismographic reactions to society's shifts in mood and taste, that is further evidence of the indestructibility of his genius.

This renowned observer of human nature made twofold use of his gift: artistically, by giving the characters in his plays a reality unequaled in the plays of his

models and most of his rivals; and professionally, by constantly keeping his finger on the pulse of his age so that he never lost contact with it and thus avoided becoming an outsider and thereby unsuccessful. There were dogmatists who reproached him for betraying his talent: where is artistic integrity among all those plays and spectacles commissioned by the court, among all those prose farces hastily written for the play-factory at the Palais Royal, among all those flowery and obsequious dedications to royal patrons?

But such criticism comes from the perspective of a later romantic and subjective age. Whether Molière himself was subjective and egocentric is very questionable. He is described as being a very sociable (if not very talkative) person. His plays stress the social nature of man, which necessarily includes the ability to compromise with existing reality. He certainly considers the inflexible Alceste (in *The Misanthrope*) to be a comic figure, although possibly right from the abstract perspective of pure idealism. The deep-rooted realism which directed Molière's talent towards comedy as its most inherently appropriate medium caused him to fail dismally when he attempted tragedy— particularly as an actor. Much to the regret of those who would have liked to have more "great comedies" from him, this realism determined the road he was to travel. Since it first of all demanded that Molière please the public (*plaire le public*), he either skillfully avoided all overwhelming obstacles or merely diplomatically noted them in passing. Survival was more important than ideology.

Ultimately, Molière usually had his way. He was a

skillful maneuverer and as a polemicist superior to
nearly everyone who picked a quarrel with him. He
knew how to come to terms with those people who
were most useful to him; he was sociable and did not
obstinately hold to any one alternative. Art has many
possibilities; if one does not work out, then the artist
tries another. If you are in a hurry, you reach back for
some proven recipe for success. You refrain from
shocking the public by confronting it with something
entirely new; instead, you almost imperceptibly blend
deeper meaning into apparently harmless jokes. Behind
cheerful superficial brilliance, a dramatist may reveal
wider and more profound dimensions which sometimes only later ages understand. In this way his contemporaries, concerned only with entertainment, perceive no attack upon their way of life. They may even
occasionally be brought to the point of unconsciously
laughing at themselves.

In this fashion Molière sailed over the dangerous
reefs that have prevented writers of comedy in all ages
from practicing their difficult profession without hindrance. While he did not completely escape these dan-
gers, he was never entirely shipwrecked. He made the
bourgeoisie laugh, although the bourgeois was the
chief object of attack in his comedies; he made the
court laugh, although it required the greatest refine-
ments for its entertainment; he remained creatively
inexhaustible, although he often repeated himself—
with subtle modifications, to be sure; he made fun of
his age without alienating himself from it and without
damning it completely; he indulged in the most tren-
chant language without losing his humanity; he showed

no signs of weariness although he often suffered from the pressures of time and from overwork; he rejuvenated himself by setting himself new tasks or by allowing others to set them for him; and he remained true to himself even when, like Proteus, he constantly transformed himself.

We do not know why Molière wrote individual plays, the inspiration for which may have come from some autobiographical impulse, or from an idea suggested to him by another play, or from something he had read, or from some observation which he had made. But we do know what he thought about his art in general. He recorded some of his fundamental aesthetic opinions in various prefaces to his printed works and, above all, in the two polemical plays written during the long controversy surrounding *The School for Wives: The Critique of The School for Wives* and *The Versailles Impromptu*. In these plays, written for specific occasions, he defended himself against scholars who accused him of disregarding dramatic rules; against precious snobs and religious zealots who found his plays (particularly his latest one) vulgar, inartistic, and blasphemous; and against the *grands comédiens* of the Hôtel de Bourgogne, who even jealously criticized Molière's acting style.

Molière's position is simple with regard to the classical rules, which had been pedantically formulated by theoreticians in the tradition of Aristotle and Horace, and mindlessly applied to every play: if these rules are of use to the play, well and good. He noted that these "few cursory observations which reason has decreed concerning those elements which might interfere with our enjoyment of a particular type of poetic work" were not mysterious absolutes but rules made by men for men. If a play which has not kept strictly to the rules pleases its audience, so much the worse for the rules, since the rule of rules is that a play must please its audience. "Do these pedants really intend to tell the public to ignore this precept so that it may no longer judge for itself what it enjoys?"

Then as now, practicing artists and critics got into each other's hair. The pedants made no attempt to judge each play according to its own intrinsic merits or theatrical effectiveness. Why was it, Molière asked, that plays written according to the rules do not succeed with the public? Do these plays betray a lack of feeling for the theater or for the demands of their age? Are the rules more a hindrance than a help? Molière followed the rules only when they suited him: the rule of the three unities, the rule dictating a three-phase structure of drama (exposition, complication, denouement), and the rule decreeing the use of verse for exalted subjects and prose for more common ones. His own conception of the theater, which was directed towards simplicity and comprehensibility, gave rise to a natural classicism that allowed for considerable flexibility. As a writer of comedies he was naturally permitted more freedom than was granted to writers of tragedies. Nevertheless the academics felt that Molière sinned against two rules in particular: indifferent to the purity of genre, he mixed farce with elegant comedy; in addition, he combined—triumphantly—

the high arts of music and dance with the lower art of farce in a form of his own invention, the ballet-comedy.

His practical theatrical experience led Molière to understand Aristotle's dictum that the drama must have a plot in a way that differed from the scholar's interpretation. Only in the rarest cases does he make use of external action and imitation of life in his plays. Artificial intrigue dominates the farces while the dramatic portrait dominates the great comedies which must make do with a minimum of external action. In *The Critique of The School for Wives* Molière defends himself against the reproach that his plays suffered from a non-Aristotelian lack of action by characterizing the reports and confessions of his *dramatis personae* as internal action. We owe to Molière the introduction of psychological depth to a genre in which the portrayal of inner activity had been completely neglected in favor of the presentation of external situations designed to create surprise.

Molière understood the comical drama of human life as arising from conflict in social and personal relationships. This approach was in opposition to the traditional view of comedy, which called for the execution of mere surprises in plot by superficially delineated characters. Molière's credo is simple but demanding in the utmost sense, as he himself was well aware: comedy deals with mankind, with the ridiculousness and with the weaknesses "*de tout le monde*" (of everybody). These weaknesses must be presented in an amiable manner, but also "*d'après nature*" (as they are in life). "The writer of tragedies," says Molière, "is free to follow the expanding flights of his imagination in its efforts to reach the realm of the marvelous, often leaving reality in the lurch in this process." The writer of comedy, on the other hand, must produce life-like portraits in which we can recognize "the people of our own age." While the former needs only reasonable ideas and greatness of style, the latter needs broad knowledge of human nature, a feeling for both the genuine and the spurious currents of his age, and the very, very rare ability "to make respectable people laugh." A comedy is a "public mirror" in which an age's general customs and morals are artistically reflected. Only rarely does this mirror reflect individual persons. "Therefore, let us not immediately refer all the details of such a comedy's general review of morality to ourselves, but let us make use of the play's moral as best as we can without revealing that we know that the play is addressing us."

Comedy must first of all please. Please whom? The audience, says Molière, *l'honnête homme*, whether he be a courtier, a burgher, or a man of the people. And then comedy is there *"pour corriger les moeurs"* (to improve morals). This is a proposition handed down from classical antiquity and repeated by Molière in his preface to *Tartuffe*, but from tactical necessity rather than deep conviction. Both of these aspects demand that the comic writer portray the men of his own age, and through these, perhaps man in general. "It is impossible for Molière," says Molière through the mouth of Bréant in *The Versailles Impromptu*, "to depict a character whose counterpart cannot be found in real life"—precisely because he writes about his own age. This involves a danger not known to the tragic writer, who places his characters in past or mythological times and designs an imaginary social life for them. In spite of the fact that he repeatedly stressed the general and fictitious nature of his protagonists Molière nearly brought ruin upon himself many times, especially when his models were recognizable and well-known in real life. The source of his greatness was also an Achilles heel vulnerable to his opponents. His portraits were so good (if not exactly flattering), that people were abashed to see themselves reflected in the mirror of his comedies.

The essential fact about Molière's art was his commitment to portraying his own times. Molière's famous "comic realism" is intimately bound up with the multi-layered social environment into which he was born and in which he lived. The most distinctive element of his work, it is even more significant than his brilliant joining of the three cornerstones of his art: the Italian *commedia dell'arte*, the popular French farce, and the comedy of classical antiquity. Because Molière was such a close observer of his environment, he was able to endow the traditional stereotypical figures of popular and literary comedy with so much life that they became contemporaries. Out of timeless types he created people recognizable to his own age. The burgher, the peasant, the nobleman, husbands and wives, parents and children appeared on stage, clothed like their counterparts in the audience; they illustrated and spoke of the same feelings and problems that preoccupied people on the streets or in the houses of Paris. The place of action is France, Paris, the present.

Only rarely, and then only transparently disguised is the scene Naples (in *Scapin*), Spain (*Don Juan*) or, in the case of the court plays, a mythological Somewhere. Molière's plays gain from their reference to a concrete world known to the audience. Amphitryon and Don Juan are in Molière's theater the contemporaries and compatriots of Alceste and Tartuffe; their customs, language, and ideas are rooted in the same soil. They were all probably dressed in costumes cut according to the current fashion.

The contemporaneous nature of Molière's plays is one of their greatest charms. Mysteriously enough, plays which were contemporary to their own day require only a change of costume to seem so to any age. And this is precisely because his plays, like all great works, address themselves to the universal by making use of the contemporary particulars in dealing with human passions and relationships, with the difficulties of communication, with problems of authority and identity, and, above all, with the illusions behind which man barricades himself against reality and against himself.

In his own theater, Molière so skillfully met the demand that dramatic characters be formed "according to nature," that for centuries his greatness was ascribed to the verisimilitude of his characters. However, a closer look makes it clear that even though his figures impress us as being unusually realistic and contemporary, they are first and foremost dramatic creations whose reality depends upon the theater, the scene, and the play in which they appear. Their greatest strength is not *vraisemblance*, verisimilitude, but rather *bienséance*, their ability to fit into the poetic scheme of an entire play. They arise from the exaggeration, stylization, and simplification of reality. Like every dramatist (but better than most of his contemporaries or successors who wrote comedy), Molière was able, with the help of theatrical illusion, to make the spectator believe that he and those like him were parading before him there on the stage. Molière's stage figures are not naturalistic but natural. He substituted multi-dimensional characters for the traditional stiff masks responsible for flat, grotesque figures endowed with very few individual qualities. While Molière stressed the essentially "comic" qualities of these more complex characters, he also rounded them out with complementary "normal" characteristics. As he wrote in *The Critique of The School for Wives*: "It is by no means inconceivable that a man can appear ridiculous in certain matters but completely worthy of respect in others."

In comedies of character, the hero's specific monomania (such as avarice, snobbishness, hypocrisy, conceit, or dogmatism) forms the comic center of the play, providing both its theme and its motor force. Around this monomania are arranged the presumptuous mask-like attitudes of the pedants, the affected snobs, the coquettes, the prudes, the impostors, the would-be wits, and those who are too good to be true. By exaggerating them either satirically or farcically, Molière renders them all ridiculous in the course of the play. Egotism is the driving force behind the maniacal passions and presumptions; and the *grimace* is the fashionable manner of expressing one's social alienation when the natural personality has been abandoned. One claims to be more than one is, but the portraitist shows us the cracks in the artificial mask and allows instinct to break through artifice so that the mute, pitiable, underdeveloped Self can flicker through. A character's presumption is rendered ridiculous when he unconsciously reveals it to the spectator.

By simultaneously stylizing the people of his own age and presenting them on the stage in a theatrically natural fashion, Molière made a discovery both for himself and for us: all life is a comedy. As the modern French dramatist Jean Anouilh writes: "We can hurt ourselves, betray ourselves, slaughter ourselves, blow ourselves up to presumptuous heights; nevertheless, we are laughable and nothing else, all of us, even those whom we call our heroes. Let the insipid philosophers of despair take note: we are laughable. And this fact is, strictly speaking, much more horrifying than these philosophers' portrayal of our unreality. Thanks to Molière the true French drama is the only place where no masses are said, but where we can laugh, laugh . . . about our own misery and our own horror. This daring act of bravado is one of France's great revelations to the world. For this we thank you, Sir." Molière's comedies create humor from disconsolation and amusement from an exhibit of egotism and wickedness. He seems to do this almost effortlessly, but we know from his own words (in *The Critique*) and from the history of the theater, how difficult a feat this is. Very few dramatists either before or after him succeeded in creating this kind of comedy despite many efforts and considerable talent.

Like everything of a dramatic nature, comedy rests upon a dialectic: the play grows out of a position and its opposite. For the thickening and unraveling of the dramatic plot, comedy has from antiquity on made use of two types in dialectical opposition: the fool and the villain, the dupe and the intriguer. Molière's work reflects this basic principle on various levels. In pure farce, this dialectic receives completely fanciful treatment. For instance, a prankster (Scapin, Mascarille, or Sbrigani), a servant, a group of young people, or a series of allies put a stop to the proceedings either of one fool or of a group of foolish figures. By inventively exploiting the fool's weaknesses and whims, they put an obstacle in the path of his harmful activity. In such cases comedy arises from both malicious joy and relief: fools such as conceited burghers and doctors, domestic or marital tyrants, must be punished in art (if not always in life)—above all, when they harm others or behave arrogantly to them. This punishment, whether achieved through the primitive means of a beating or through more sophisticated ones, such as the prevention of an "unnatural" marriage, of disinheritance, or of the suppression of children and dependents, generates amusement because the restoration of order is gratifying and removes anxiety.

Molière's farces and comedies all more or less follow this obvious and well-tried pattern. One character becomes the victim of an intrigue because his specific weaknesses hinder a group of characters—who are dependent upon or in some way involved with him— from pursuing their own natural interests. The victim never learns from experience: ridiculous characters are incapable of learning in this manner, for one of their weaknesses is always unreasonableness, lack of insight, and unresponsiveness in the face of attempts to persuade them of their folly. Thus every "ridiculous" character really becomes the victim of his own weakness or presumption. The victim becomes isolated, confused, and finally rendered harmless. The intrigue lures him either into a net that he himself has spun or into a trap that stubborness has prevented him from seeing; it snaps shut before he is aware of it, leaving him helpless to defend himself. The intriguers play on the keyboard of his weaknesses like a virtuoso on his instrument; they do not think out a plan from A to Z, but rather they improvise. As in a chess game where the players' moves and countermoves are as much a matter of improvisation as of calculation—in the hope but not the certainty of a fortunate outcome—so, too, are the improvised moves of the intriguers. Every move has its own poetic causality that either fells a victim or grotesquely makes him hang a noose around his own neck, which is often very loosely tied. This increasing predicament is dependent upon accidental occurrences and is made still more inescapable by many surprises (both ancient elements of comedy), so that the spectator is held in a state of breathlessness and cheerful tension.

The happy end of comedy—which is no mirror of life, but rather a convention of poetic justice—is not always achieved by means of the pranksters' intrigues against the principal guilty figure. As in a chess game, the players are sometimes maneuvered into a position from which they cannot escape. *Tartuffe, The Miser,* and *The School for Wives* all reach an impasse, and it temporarily appears that in the drama, as in life, no happy end is foreseeable. In order to achieve a happy conclusion, Molière then uses a device which readers have frequently deplored but which actors have praised, because it is so gloriously playable. Like the writers of tragedy whom Molière had criticized, he retreated into the realm of the marvelous and resorted to helpful intervention from outside (for example, the King's messenger in *Tartuffe*). He also organizes a miraculous clarification of identities so that those people who have been separated find one another again, thus allowing those wished-for but obstructed unions to take place at last. The comedy, having reached an impasse with its realistic criticism of customs and vices, is thus transformed into a wonderful fairy tale in which all turns out for the best.

This transformation functions properly only if we at all times remember that we are witnessing a play —in other words, a work which must have a beginning and an end in accordance with the rules of art. Thus the work must, of course, differ from life. By means of these miraculous conclusions "pasted" onto the work, the dramatist consciously breaks through the illusion of verisimilitude and ironically affirms the principles of his craft. The creator shapes the creatures of his imagination according to his own purposes.

Molière found yet another way out of the comic writer's eternal dilemma. Where some final joke did not finish off a tightly woven dramatic conflict, or

where a *deus ex machina* was not used to resolve a
dramatic conflict heading for catastrophe, Molière
simply allowed his play to remain unresolved in a
dialectical sense. In such cases he concluded with a
dance, a masquerade, or a ballet-round in which the
leitmotives were put through their drills once again—
grotesquely and in pantomime—and were then dissolved into the realm of fantasy. Art is once again
allowed to hold its own and dominate the stage; that is
to say, the art of the theater itself is emphasized
through the playwright's grandiose deployment of
purely theatrical devices.   1748228

Thus Molière is not only a master in the comic art
of characterization, he is also a master of form. He
maintains control of his composition both in its details
and in their reference to the whole—from the smallest
contribution to dramatic study of a scene to the total
configuration of a play. He is by choice neither an
experimentalist nor a perfectionist.

Many of Molière's contemporaries angrily accused
him of plagiarism and pointed out that his themes,
plots, and comic situations had often already been used
elsewhere. "*Je prends mon bien ou je le trouve*" (I
take what belongs to me wherever I find it) was his
maxim, and it was offered without shame or apology.
His many years of practical stage experience, especially
during the time of his apprenticeship in the provinces, had provided him with a wealth of conventions
and traditions which he drew upon freely whenever
he needed material. Research of Molière's sources
would show that all his plays could be analyzed in
terms of his "predecessors." Most of them can be

traced to several sources: Plautus and Terence, chap-books, Boccaccio, the Spanish theatrical tradition, the Italian tradition of both folk and elegant theater, the works of French contemporaries—all were godfathers to his dramas at one time or another (and sometimes all together). In his own words, he took what he needed wherever he found it. More than once he took what he needed from his own work: a series of well-tried scenes appear with slight variations in different plays; earlier works—now lost to us—are polished and revised until they are entirely new plays. The drama-tist is a sleight-of-hand artist continually constructing new entities from similar parts.

Like Shakespeare or Brecht, the dramatist pressured for time does not worry himself over invention; com-position and interpretation keep him sufficiently busy. Thus his artistic personality is conveyed not so much by the building blocks themselves as by their selection and combination. The borrowed material is given a new reality; the dramatist's own experience, first, of the stage and second, of mankind, directs his creative process. Thus Molière so changes and improves his "pilfered" material that it becomes entirely his own. In this fashion heterogeneous elements are welded to-gether to form what appears to be a seamless whole —if not for the academicians, who feel that they must continually attack this most unacademic of French comic writers with their red pencils, then at least for the spectator in the theater. This genius, sensitive to his very fingertips, offers the man in the audience a unified drama that is unmistakably his own.

What do we mean by an unacademic writer of

comedy? Molière is considered to be a classicist, a member of that brilliant constellation of three which includes the tragedians Corneille and Racine (the one a decade older, the other a decade younger than Molière). He is thought to be representative of the seventeenth century's high ideals: reason, order, and clarity. The form of his comedies is doubtless directed by these ideals, not, as mentioned above, in the academic sense of an adherence to rules and schemes, but rather in the practical sense of structural simplicity and transparency—even where complex psychological problems are involved. His plays are "reasonable" and they are functionally organized. This is true whether they describe the continuous curve of a dramatic intrigue, or shape a dramatic portrait in terms of a theme with variations, or sketch the progressive convolutions of a comedy of manners—the three typical forms of Molière's comedy. Reason, or more precisely, *bon sens* (common sense) is the rule which Molière obeys: there are no ramified complications, no digressions, but rather an organization focusing on one figure, one couple, or on one theme about which all the other figures and situations revolve. The organization is loose in *Don Juan*, episodic in *The Would-Be Gentleman*, and built upon duplication in *Amphitryon*. This organization can be very symmetrical where, for example, the various groupings, each having a different value within the play, are arranged according to the degree of their ridiculousness.

When themes vary from play to play they are provided a background by the more or less constant theme of frustrated love. The comic character is mea-

sured against this theme, which represents a test he is
never able to pass. This is actually the theme of youth
searching for happiness in a world badly administered
by crotchety, egotistical, vice-ridden adults. The love
of the daughters and sons of these stubborn burghers
for the sons and daughters of similarly stubborn burghers is extremely fragile and beset with danger from
all sides. Above all, it is subordinate to the will and
wishes of all-powerful fathers who, though they may
be sure of themselves, are far from sure of achieving
their goals. In their foolishness the elders are blind to
the feelings of these young people; unable to comprehend the happiness generated by human relationships
entered into freely and on the basis of mutual attraction, they attempt in their folly to impose upon moving young girls unlovable and unloving suitors—
impostors and intriguers, fools and dowry hunters,
lascivious old men and ambitious snobs. A situation is
thereby created in which filial love comes sharply into
conflict with the natural feelings these girls have for
their chosen lovers, youths of their own age.

In its treatment of this ancient comic theme, Molière's theater borders on the tragic. For it is here that
he demonstrates the worthlessness of a society whose
authorities, forgetting their own youth, egotistically
misuse their prerogatives to dominate the conduct of
the young. This is the greatest of the adult vices and
appears as a regular accompaniment to an assortment
of manias that vary from case to case. Whether this
mania be Orgon's striving for a holy life, Argan's
hypochondriacal self-centeredness, Harpagon's love of
money, or Arnolphe's and Sganarelle's dogmatism,

these egotistical men all threaten the right to life, happiness, and independence of those young people who are under their thumb. With childlike gracefulness or ferocious cruelty, with energy and with a wealth of ingenuity, the young in turn fight to the end for their rights.

Why did Molière emphasize this contrapuntal activity so strongly? Is it more than just an artistic pretext, a way of providing a base for plots rich in episode, a useful background against which he can develop a comic portrait? Is counterpoint perhaps the basis of his theater, its leitmotif? Does it represent both his conception of human happiness and wisdom, and the essence of his dramatic poetry? It is as if he wished to say over and over again: this is the good life with which we must not interfere; those who belong together according to the decrees of nature and affection must find each other. Those who do not voluntarily accept this point of view—even though it may partially conflict with their own interests—must expect to meet with opposition, intrigue, tenacious resistance.

Molière's young people are victorious at the end, although usually by the skin of their teeth. They have only been touched by the shadow of tragedy. In their struggle for survival, they have sharpened their claws and have learned all sorts of useful—if perhaps nasty—tricks; they have contravened bourgeois virtues and have neglected their filial duty. In so doing, they are given a foretaste of their own fate as adults. But for the present they are still young and nature is on their side. The counterpoint ends in a cheerful major chord: *amor vincit omnia*—love conquers all, at least in art through the cheerfulness of comedy.

The love of these young people takes into consideration the concept of a balanced life as well as overall personality. It has nothing to do with the infatuation or lasciviousness of the old lovers who seize upon the wrong object and become blinded by their passion or self-love. The young people may sulk a bit, flirt from time to time, have moods, or momentarily doubt one another. But what they want is right, and they deserve to get it. The goal is always marriage and eternal constancy, not merely the bedroom and sensual thrills, not pleasure (*le plaisir*) but happiness (*le bonheur*).

Molière is almost the only one of the time-honored writers of comedy and farce to remain—firmly though effortlessly—within the bounds of propriety when dealing with love. His comedy sparkles without the traditional sexual allusions and ambiguities which spice later French farces. Such allusions are the *sine qua non* of classical comedy, and they are also deeply embedded in Shakespeare's multilevel comic language.

Only when dealing with the theme of the cuckold does Molière venture into that area of sexual allusion, which he despised. Even then, he does so not for the sake of sexual titillation as such, but because it is in this very area that the *barbon bourgeois* (the bourgeois graybeard) is especially vulnerable. Sganerelle, Arnolphe, Georges Dandin all fear that they will be cuckolded, and this fear springs from their narcissism and conceit, as well from their peculiar attitude toward women. For these graybeards, cuckoldom is much the same as being victimized by theft, since wives are personal possessions not to be distinguished from sacks of money, titles, and the abused privileges of authority. With this attitude the bourgeois condemns himself: he is absolutely incapable of loving, that is to say, he does not recognize the right to individual existence of a person but sees a person only as an object serving his own interests. Since he cannot comprehend a relationship based on genuine feeling for a woman, there is naturally no equality of rights in a physical sense.

The woman defends herself through coquetry (if she is still young) and through prudery (when she is older). She pleads and struggles for independence, proper education, and the free choice of a partner—if her heart is in the right place. In any case, she opposes the tyrannical and absolute rule of the autocratic male. In his comedies Molière, like Shakespeare, always sides with the young women. Active, quick-witted, independent girls are well-suited to comedy; through them comedy is able to deal a blow at those men who strut through God's creation as proud as peacocks; the result is the establishment of a cheerful balance between the sexes, an equilibrium not found in life. Comedy, at least, can create an amusing tug-of-war.

However, Molière is concerned with two more serious matters: first, the destruction of the protagonist's dogmatic exercise of authority and, second, the individual's rejection of an arbitrarily assigned role which threatens to destroy his personality. No one may harm another person for the sake of his own interests, and no genuine personal relationship is possible between partners who do not share similar interests and rights—above all the right to bestow one's affections freely. Thus Molière's comedies reveal examples of vice, not in the vulgar sense, but as demonstrations of sins against humanity: somebody feels himself to be superior to others and does not permit these others to consider their own interests at all; or, somebody values material things or the "salvation" of his soul more than he values his own family and dependents.

The sin against mankind is, in a word, egotism which finds a different embodiment in each of Molière's plays. Whatever its form, this egotism severely disrupts the functioning of that social unit or miniature world in which the egotist finds himself at home and in a position of dominance. Molière not only shows us the forms of this disruption but its effect upon the disturber himself; for he is his own worst enemy. His egotism isolates him so that he finally stands alone in Alceste's desert. Unloved and unable to make contact with others, he is condemned to his own company. He has betrayed man's naturally social nature and is not, therefore, an *honnête homme* in Molière's sense. One could weep for him, if in his lack of insight and in his conflict between will and instinct he were not so laughable, if he were not so easy to dupe, such an easy prey to flattery, and so easily provoked to anger. A man who must always be right, who can never be taught anything, and who is as inflexible as a wooden puppet, is outwitted like the blockhead he really is. In a nature which might possibly be noble and good some part of the personality has become thoroughly rotten. This would be pitiable if it were not so funny.

Around this principal comic figure dance rings of ridiculous pedants and *poseurs* who have similarly forfeited their humanity. Boastful pedanticism, doctrinaire aestheticism, and constant imitation of fashions in dress and speech have destroyed their personal substance and social responsibility. They have all become dessicated caricatures of human beings at whom one can only laugh, although what they do is really so sad.

By devising a contrast, Molière gives a sharp profile to this whole mad world of conceited egotists, a world which is everywhere out of joint. He puts on stage a figure who—by commenting, philosophizing, and discussing—represents a different and ideal dimension, the dimension of *raison* (reason). And here we come to the essence of this great French master.

However, his intent is not quite as simple as some early critics have claimed: the *raisonneur* who constantly preaches reason (Ariste, Chrysalde, Philinte, Cléante, Béralde) is not Molière's direct mouthpiece and his opinions are by no means to be simply taken as Molière's practical wisdom randomly served up. To do so would be to misunderstand greatly Molière's conception of his dramatic craft. The *raisonneur* of the great comedies has primarily a dramatic function. Molière's opinions, however, are not put into his mouth like abstract *bons mots* on the subjects of the *juste milieu* (the golden mean), *traitabilité* (tractability), avoidance of excess, the rights of the majority, conformity to society, and the stoic acceptance of existing situations. Rather, these opinions form a concrete part of the play as a whole; they are the opinions of a dramatist and not those of an abstract philosopher. They are concrete demonstrations of the dramatist's view of human relationships, human behavior, and the functioning of social units. They are not meant to serve as methodical instruction or as a guidebook for proper conduct—as quoted wisdom, so to speak.

On closer analysis, the guidance which Sganarelle, Arnolphe, Orgon, Alceste, and Argan receive from their reasonable or sophistic relatives and friends turns out to be not a matter of general rules of conduct but only the exact opposite of what the comic protagonists practice in their own lives. The *raisonneur* is a stereotypical figure only in his broadest outlines and in his general function. When it comes down to details, his sermons, his concepts of reason and of common sense are different in each case. The somewhat insipid *raisonneur*-philosophy of moderation and adaptability runs the gamut all the way from practical empiricism to a superficial inclination to compromise. His voice provides that variation of the comic theme which represents accommodation and a putting in order. The moral it preaches is never an absolute; it is always determined by the social context presented in the play.

The concepts of reason, nature, and common sense, which each *raisonneur* uses according to his own definition, shimmer in all the colors of the rainbow; in each case, however, the color is complementary to that which characterizes the hero himself. The *raisonneur* therefore does not represent Molière's own moral intentions; Molière has no specific moral intentions. At most his plays present moral implications: if a person behaves in this or that manner, it is unreasonable; the reasonable thing to do in his position would be to act as the *raisonneur* suggests. Molière does not expressly adhere to the traditional notion as put forward in the preface to *Tartuffe*—that the comedy is there *pour corriger les moeurs* solely through the judicious speeches of the *raisonneur* (who sometimes makes suggestions which are not morally irreproachable). Instead, Molière demonstrates his point by means of a rich dramatic panorama of mores and by having the principal guilty figure punished at the end of the play.

The *raisonneur* is therefore more appropriately considered a dramatic figure as corrective or contrast to the protagonist; he draws out the latter's opinions through conversation and serves as a passive foil by means of which the portrait of the fool is sharply outlined. In addition, he also mediates between the public and the action taking place on the stage: he informs us in a prophetic manner of the workings of the plot and of the conclusion of the play; he puts things in order, clarifies, and affirms so that we may better understand (*pour mieux entendre*). He is there in the interest of the symmetry and clarity of the dramatic event.

It is a relief to realize that Molière was no mild liberal, an ever-compromising social being of Philinte's or Cléante's sort. He believed in the contradictory nature of man and knew that conflicts between the individual and society were necessary. He accepted the primacy of society but was not always happy about existing conditions. (One need only think of *The Misanthrope*, in which the ruling society is rather sharply condemned and the *raisonneur* Philinte plays a very ambivalent role as mediator.)

If Molière has any advice to give us in his plays as a whole and not through one figure alone, it is this: in the nature of things man lives in a community, sometimes in an evil one. It is necessary to make concessions to this community and to respect certain rules of the game even when, as sometimes occurs, one's humanity thereby suffers a loss. The important thing is survival. Compromise is preferable to stubborn insistence upon the right for the sake of an unrealizable ideal, particularly when this harms others—and perhaps even oneself. Human behavior consists of give and take; conflicts are inevitable. It is better to have an imperfect society than none at all. Whoever fails to recognize this is comical. He could also be tragic, although in the final analysis Molière does not see things in this light. He shows us what is true and what is real: human nature, will, instinct, reason, and the nature of society. He does not show us ideals—not what should be, but what is.

What holds true for the moral aspects of Molière's work also holds true for the autobiographical elements: one can never actually take hold of them, for they are implied and infinitely transformed in the work. One might cite, for example, *The School for Wives*, in which many claimed to see in Arnolphe and Agnès portraits of Molière and Armande—his wife, and twenty years his junior. Since Molière played

Arnolphe and Armande played Agnès, the age difference probably determined the choice of theme. Many
parallels can be drawn, but the comic and dramatic
refractions of personal experience are so manifold that
precise conclusions are impossible.

Nor are they necessary. What matters is the objective achievement of the play and not the subjective
raw material that has been consumed in its creation.
Concerning this raw material there can only be conjecture, not certainty. First, there are the reports of
Molière's friends as recorded by his first and not entirely reliable biographer. (When Grimarest describes
the difficult marriage of the Molières—so different
in both age and temperament—he does so more according to his own convictions than in keeping with
biographical exactness.) Second, there are some traditional tales of Molière's confessions—probably apocry-
phal—concerning his poor choice in marriage and
the passionate nature of his unrequited love.

We do not know for sure what made an actor out
of a bourgeois, nor do we know how Molière understood this or that episode in his life. There are only the
dry, ambiguous facts of a work-filled existence, a life
which became progressively more difficult toward its
end, a life in which success aroused great opposition,
and in which the glittering favor of the King led to
envy from Molière's rivals and hostility from those
who opposed the King. Though the plays themselves
provide a precise portrait of the personality of the artist, they offer only an indirect one of the man. As they
were intended to do, the plays depicted the men of
Molière's time, and through them, men of all times.

Similarities between the figures and situations in the plays and in Molière's life are not accidental, but the degree of artistic transformation is so great and so complicated that no certain conclusions can be drawn. Generations of scholars have succeeded in reaching nothing more conclusive than conjecture: Molière's objectivity as a writer was stronger than his urge to confess. We know as little (or as much) of his inner life as we know of Shakespeare's; for this inner life is dispersed in a distilled form throughout his plays.

The external skeleton of his life as a director, business man, and courtier is better documented. We have the troupe's ledgers in which every performance is listed by Molière's faithful actor and bookkeeper, La Grange, according to its receipts, expenses, and cast. We also have petitions to the King and to other influential persons, and we have the polemical writings for and against Molière which accompanied the scandals surrounding the plays from *The Precious Damsels* on.

The comic or tragic aspects of his theatrical career are a matter of record. His existence as an artist meant everything to him: the playwright and the actor in him came first. They came before the moralist, the philosopher, the father, the lover, and also before the man who had fallen seriously ill. When Boileau tried to persuade his friend to give up acting in order to conserve his failing health, Molière refused: the theater was his life; as long as he lived he had to write, act, and produce plays. On the very last afternoon of his life, an attempt was made to persuade him to remain at home and not to act that evening. But what would become of all the other actors? They would lose their day's wages! He went through with the performance and collapsed onstage. His last breath of life was dedicated to the theater.

Theater must have been a true passion for Molière, for he made infinite sacrifices to it: the comforts of bourgeois life, his social position, and perhaps his health as well. (The contemporary actor's position as a social outsider is indicated by the story of Molière's nighttime interment—although to some extent that event may be traced to the rumors of godlessness that accompanied the *Tartuffe* scandal.)

The actor and the playwright are so intermingled in this man that the two functions cannot be separated. It is a combination seldom found in other dramatists. It not only explains Molière's eminently gesture-laden language, but—more importantly—the way in which he artistically organized scenes, acts, and whole units of plays in the interest of an entire theatrical event, and his readiness to adopt traditional situations that had already proved theatrically successful. It also explains Molière's transformation of experience into dramatically effective material as well as the kind of simplicity and realism his comedies have if they are properly acted. And by "properly acted" is meant not productions stressing realistic illusion, but those emphasizing proper tempo, tension, and effects geared to understanding rather than to identification.

For his plays are not imitations of life but of art; they are the creations of fantasy. They are choreographic and musical; had we only once been able to see Molière himself in them, we would have seen them performed as such—that is to say, without the excessive flourishes of his contemporaries, but with a stylization which never allowed one to forget that one was in a theater and that the people on the stage were actors. As for the great Molière himself, he always remained the same, although he played Sganarelle one day, Alceste the next, and Scapin the day after that.

PLAYS

The Precious Damsels
(Les Précieuses ridicules, 1659)

Molière's career as a writer began with his third play, *The Precious Damsels* (1659), performed a few months after he had installed himself and his troupe in Paris. He had returned to the French capital after a thirteen-year apprenticeship in the provinces, and he was slowly beginning to make a name for himself as an actor, as a theater director, and as the author of farces. I used the term "writer," but this must be qualified. Like the plays that preceded and followed it, *The Precious Damsels* was written for a specific performance by Molière's own actors in his own theater. The troupe had to win a public and for this purpose new comic material was continually needed for performances. (Molière's troupe had had no real success with tragedy, although they kept on trying; the *Grands Comèdiens* of the Hôtel de Bourgogne were really better at this form.) Even in the provinces there had been a shortage of material, and Molière had developed his abilities as a writer of comedy—first out of necessity and then more and more out of a sense of sheer enjoyment.

The Precious Damsels was to be another one of these farces—a single long act divided into seventeen scenes and written in prose. The author had written in juicy burlesque roles for both himself and for the second comic, Jodelet. The premiere was a success, people came in droves, and the play had a long run. Then it occurred to someone to have the play printed without the knowledge of the author, who only learned of it after it was too late. Instead of making a fuss, however, Molière adapted himself to his new role as a writer and, although he pretended to be somewhat vexed, he was actually secretly flattered. Adaptability was something which Molière practiced throughout his life; this was particularly true if he knew that the only alternative would be a long period of irritation and if no question of principle was involved (as there was during the later controversy over *Tartuffe*). The pirate publishers included a preface by Molière in which the "inexperienced author" protested against this unfair treatment. However, the preface also vibrates with Molière's pride at the success of his play and with his faint contempt for his "learned," published colleagues into whose ranks he had now fallen through no fault of his own. He gracefully pokes fun at both his fellow playwrights and the zealous theoreticians of the theater, asserting that his own lack of theorizing was due to the pressure of time and lack of space; however, he makes it sufficiently clear that he doesn't think much of such activity.

Molière also takes this opportunity to indulge in

polemics for his own purposes. *The Precious Damsels* not only made the audience laugh, it also provoked a few wry faces. Molière vociferously protested against the occasional attacks against him. He really cannot understand, Molière argues in the preface, what these people can have against his play, for it remains completely within the bounds of honorable and permissible satire. After all, he had not attacked preciosity itself, but only its falsified and ridiculous imitation. "It has been the concern of comedy from time immemorial to expose to criticism corrupt imitations of perfection. Truly learned men and the truly brave are wrong to take the doctor or the captain of comedy amiss, as are also the good judges, princes and kings when they are angered by seeing a Trivalin or some other actor portray a judge, a prince or a king in a ridiculous manner upon the stage of a theater." These are the skillful tactics of defense: if one's opponent insists that he has been seriously attacked, he is accused of humorlessness, or even of being guilty of the same ridiculous imitation of perfection.

It is very doubtful whether Molière's defense is in this case anything more than a tactical maneuver. Given his fondness for ridicule, Molière must have been delighted to take on preciosity, even when it was genuine, as in the Parisian salons, particularly that of Madame de Rambouillet. For preciosity generally represented a very artificial social mask, a linguistic and moral affectation. It was a turning away from nature, a denial of the instincts, and a kind of superficial idealism; as such, it was precisely the stuff of which comedy is made. By depicting a pair of provincial snobs instead of their urban models, Molière does not excuse the original phenomenon; rather, he simply demonstrates that twofold ridiculousness is more effective than ridiculousness on one level. He exaggerates and stylizes, which is nothing at all new. Whether *The Precious Damsels* is considered a satire, a comedy, or a farce, all of these genres draw their life from exaggeration. No audience can be moved to laughter by means of pure naturalism.

As for another point of protest in Molière's preface, he rightly characterizes himself as an unwilling author. The text of a play provides us with only one of its aspects. Its actual performance is much more important, since Molière's plays depend to a great extent upon movement and tone of voice (*depend de l'action et du ton de voix*). The physical and not the literary structure makes the play. Thus Molière's plays are not designed to be read since the text is only an outline, a sum of cues or catchwords for actors and directors. Molière wrote *comédies d'acteur* (comedies for actors), and performed all of them himself with his own troupe. Therefore, he never thought of these plays in terms of publication. Later, with his increasing success, it became self-evident that these plays would be published, but it was never a necessity. The single necessity was performance. For this Molière was prepared to fight tenaciously—for his *Tartuffe*, for *Don Juan*, for *The Misanthrope* and for *The School for Wives*.

When Molière established himself in Paris, farce had already been absent from the theater for two decades. Only tragedies and comedies derived from the classics were performed, and neither the one nor the other was the forte of Molière's troupe. Whether they were performing in the provinces, in cities, or privately in the houses of aristocrats, Molière's troupe had always won the heart of its public with farces of Italian, Spanish and French origin. Thus it was with farce that Molière began his career as a playwright.

On his very first appearance at court, Molière had so charmed Louis XIV with a farce, that Monsieur, the King's brother, had taken over the patronage of the troupe. Now Molière wanted to win over the Parisians. He had a wonderful idea for a farce, but dressed it up as a comedy of manners, combining the traditional with the contemporary. What he did was to present to the Parisian audience a phenomenon with which it was intimately acquainted; but by employing the methods of farce he showed this phenomenon in an alienated and ridiculous form. Because it was interested in the subject being treated, this audience also renewed its taste for the methods the dramatist used. More precisely, it renewed its taste for the kind of laughter characteristic of farce. With this apparent step backwards, the man from the provinces took a decisive step forward: he made the hearty laughter of the peasants once again respectable in the bourgeois theater, and he liberated comedy from the straitjacket of an all too literary tradition.

The title—literally "the ridiculous précieuses"— provides a key to the purpose of the play: it is directed against the pretentions of preciosity, against its ridiculous aspects and not against preciosity itself. But the play does more than this, otherwise it would be simply a contemporary satire. *The Precious Damsels* actually directs itself against presumption and arrogance in general, and it illustrates the fact that comic play thrives on this very thing. It is a play of disguises, pretenses, and make-believe.

Schematically, we have a coarsely plotted intrigue. Two young suitors have been rejected by two young provincial beauties who have taken their first steps into the great world in Paris. Unfortunately the ladies have brought with them from the provinces all sorts of absurd and romantic ideas concerning everyday life. They have also been deeply infected by what they have heard about preciosity as it is practiced in the Parisian salons. The young men have evidently pressed their suit too brusquely and too directly and have thereby broken those rules which the girls have imagined must be kept to in the game of love.

The rejection must be avenged, however, since masculine pride has been deeply wounded. A drastic joke is planned: pretentiousness must be met with still greater pretentiousness. Thus two servants are sent to the girls disguised as precious Parisian snobs. As the Marquis de Mascarille and the Viscount de Jodelet, the servants win over the coy beauties by means of fine words and clothes, promises and bombast. The young men step in themselves when the joke has reached its climax. They reveal the ridiculous conspiracy, treat the girls with contempt, and beat the servants whose enthusiasm has led them to carry the joke to the point of taking themselves seriously. Those who had originally been shabbily treated end in triumph, and those who had initially triumphed end in disgrace.

What we have, then, is a consciously artificial intrigue derived from an ancient theatrical tradition which employs disguises, inversions of social rank, various types of situation comedy, and the contrast between appearance and reality. The comic aspect of the play arises from these contrasts—between persons, between the different kinds of language spoken, between the various levels (i.e., reality, game) upon which the figures operate.

In addition to the ridiculous damsels (Magdelon and Cathos) and the disguised snobs (Mascarille and Jodelet), there is also the bourgeois (Gorgibus), a farcical figure if ever there was one. He is first of all a strict father.

When he learns that the girls have rejected their suitors, he rages like an insulted *pater familias*: "I intend to be absolute master here." He is also a bourgeois who is obsessed with questions of money: "The pomades these girls use will make a beggar of me. In every nook and corner I find egg white, virgin's milk, and all sorts of unrecognizable junk. A dozen pigs have had to donate their lard to these pomades since we've been here." For Gorgibus, his daughter and niece are marriageable goods, and every suitor is immediately thought of as a potential husband. He wants the whole world to run according to dictates, but even his own flesh and blood fails to do so.

The contrast between burgher and snob is sharp. The burgher speaks of marriage as the only natural goal for a woman and thus presses for a depersonalized institution. For him there are no disgressions, no *bon ton* (good manners), no pomades, no play, and no pleasure; there are only material goods, trade and duty. It is no wonder that the girls go to the other extreme. Basically, they are solid middle-class daughters who have only assumed the most literal form of preciosity; in them conceit and reality have made an incongruous pact. The result is that these girls behave unnaturally—speaking artificially in a language which names nothing by its proper name, acting artificially with men whom they would like to force into stiff but "fine" forms of social conduct, and indulging in an artificial snobbishness which causes them to disregard their own genuine needs and to misjudge other human beings. They therefore become the all-too-easy victims of deception, since anyone catering to their notions can win them over, the pretenders rather more easily than those who are sincere.

In *The Precious Damsels* Mascarille not only appears as a servant but also as a conceited aesthete and false marquis. His preciosity, like that of the girls, represents nothing more than superficiality, but he actually wears an ingenious mask. After all, Mascarille means a small mask. This is the last time for a long while (not until *Scapin*) that Molière will play a masked character of the kind which he learned about in the provinces from the itinerant Italian actors of the *commedia dell'arte* tradition. (Incidentally, Molière shared a theater in Paris with the Italians, and on evenings when he was not performing himself he was able to watch the famous Scaramouche and learn from him all sorts of gestures and theatrical tricks.)

Mascarille is a figure of fantasy, derived from the servant and the prankster. He is fantastic first of all because of his excessively beribboned, beruffed, and brightly colored costume. He is also fantastic in his conceitedness, which allows him to fabricate titles and acts of military heroism for himself, and to pretend to enormous artistic proficiency. For example, although he has never studied music he claims to have written a history of the Roman Empire in the form of madrigals, and he mentions other musical compositions. He boasts of enjoying brilliant friendships, of having exquisite taste, and of possessing hordes of servants. In short, his is the universe of the megalomaniac, a universe created out of thin air and consisting only of the colorful shadows of reality.

As is frequently done in comedy, Molière makes use of duplication in this play (i.e., two young girls, two young men, etc.); he provides Mascarille with a counterpart—a second servant, played by the actor Jodelet whom Molière had spirited away from the Théâtre du Marais and engaged for his own troupe. Jodelet, who plays in white-face, is just as fantastically costumed and just as fantastically inventive as Mascarille. As the two girls listen breathlessly, Jodelet and Mascarille indulge in a duel of words in which they outdo one another in grandiose lies until they reach the heights of the absurd.

The scenes with Mascarille are scenes of pure farce laden with gags and jokes, but underscored with glorious verbal satire. Mascarille arrives onstage in a sedan chair and his presumptuous splendor is immediately exposed in an action of the sort frequently found in situation comedy: the one porter who has requested his fare is paid with a box on the ear, but the other porter—a "reasonable" man (*il est raisonnable*) who has threatened him with a stick (language which the servant in Mascarille understands)—is promptly paid in coin. Mascarille struts about like a peacock in his colorful feathers, lets himself be admired, tugs at himself, twists and turns. He swaggers in his speeches as well, which consist of all sorts of precious clichés and which reach ultimate absurdity through excess and exaggeration. He speaks of the "theft of his heart" and of the art of writing poems about this theft. He also produces a typically precious poem which he and the girls analyze together as if they were experts in literary criticism. This text analysis becomes a comic showpiece which Molière later repeats in other plays. By depicting the ecstasy evoked in these snobs by the fourfold repetition of the initial sigh "Oh" and the concluding cry *au voleur* (stop thief!), Molière employs exaggeration to underscore the shallow literary taste of these precious people. Mascarille sings and Mascarille dances, but it is all such a distortion of fashionable taste in art, that it makes the audience laugh. The girls are enchanted, however, since their conceit has found an embodiment in Mascarille.

The play ends with beatings and with the literal removal of the presumptuous masks: Mascarille and Jodelet are disrobed. The girls stand convicted of having taken mere appearance for reality. They have been left in the lurch by that very literature in which they had placed their faith as if it were a basic principle of life. But Mascarille himself is a fiction, as is all preciosity which strives to smarten up life by means of fiction (that is, through courtly romances, romantic games of love and euphemistic language).

In the overall, at no time is *The Precious Damsels* anything but theater, fantasy, and fiction. It consists of marionette figures and treats life as a game. The location of the play is the stage, only faintly fitted out to look like a middle-class house. The time of the play is theatrical time, various moments of one day whose intervals are indeterminate—in a word, theatrical moments. The figures move about in time and space according to the whim of the author, for it is the mechanism of the play and not the plausibility of life which regulates their entrances and exits.

The School for Husbands
(L'École des maris, 1661)
  and
The School for Wives
(L'École des femmes, 1662)

Molière has added a whole series of new figures to the literature of the theater. These are in part derivations from traditional characters, in part characterizations of his own "contemporaries" transformed into stage figures, and in part the pure creatures of his own imagination. It is interesting to observe how many of these figures grow out of one another in the course of time. The characters of both the folk tradition and the classical tradition undergo manifold variations and, while still preserving the outlines of their original form, they are rounded out by the dramatist: combined with the attributes of other characters, or augmented by the dramatist's own observations of life. The *commedia dell'arte* and the French folk tradition, which were themselves popularizations of the classical tradition of comedy, provided Molière with the burgher, the doctor, the

62

nobleman, the young lovers, and the servant. But he has individualized these figures, adapted them to the immediate situation, freed them from their rigid typicality, and humanized them.

Molière was the greatest comic actor of his age. In nearly every play there is a role which he himself portrayed, and which was generally the comic, grotesque, and burlesque center of the play. While some of its characteristics remained constant, this figure inevitably underwent a metamorphosis during the twenty-five years of its creator's career as an actor and playwright. The first of the line was Mascarille, who appeared in the early plays as a servant and prankster.

A disguised marionette and the descendent of Harlequin, he was always an entirely theatrical figure whose function was to make people laugh. Behind his mask lay the virtuoso actor whose mimicry and gesture suggested the art practiced by the popular acrobats and clowns seen at annual country fairs. Mascarille then becomes Sganarelle, who no longer wears a mask but who still retains a suggestion of disguise with his moustache, his overly large eyebrows, and his yellow-green costume. As a character Sganarelle is more flexible than Mascarille, now a burgher (in *The School for Husbands*), now again a servant (in *Don Juan*), here a main character and there a second fiddle, constantly changing from play to play. Ultimately, Sganarelle becomes Scapin who is no longer the victim of other people's pranks or of his own conceit and stubbornness, but an ingenious spirit who causes great confusion, who is comprehensible to no one and taken in by no one.

In *The Imaginary Cuckold*, Sganarelle begins his career as a comically conceited man, a petty bourgeois who suspects his wife of unfaithfulness, though his suspicions have no foundation other than his own mistrust. The cuckold is a classical comic figure; the conceited cuckold is twice as comical, for illusion and comical reality are intermingled in this play. In *The School for Husbands*, his next play, Molière is concerned not merely with false appearances and credulity, but rather with a form of conceit which is still more fundamental and more vicious: Sganarelle suffers from dogmatic obstinacy, from the obdurate idea that he can have his own way, although his wishes contradict the customs of his age and the natural feelings of those who are dependent upon him. He is a reactionary burgher, a generation behind in his prejudices and in his ideals. He cannot and will not adapt, but must, however, yield to the progressive majority, becoming ridiculous in the process.

Approximately two years later, *The School for Husbands* was provided with a companion piece, *The School for Wives*. Sganarelle himself no longer appears in this play, but Arnolphe, a hopeful candidate for marriage, represents his logical continuation and is a deeper and more fully rounded character. Both plays focus upon the *education des filles* (the education of young girls), which is one of Molière's main themes and one which has preserved its freshness even today. In both instances, Molière passes judgment on his comic hero in the same way, and in both plays he works out a contrast in which the progressive idea of education stands in opposition to a reactionary concept.

The first play makes use of a traditional form of comic duplication with its somewhat mechanical symmetry and superficial plot intrigue: two girls, two old men, and, finally, two marriages. The second *School* does without such duplication. In this work, the dramatist has concentrated his interest upon creating a greater depth of characterization and upon intensifying interpersonal relationships. With it, Molière created his first great comedy of character; in Arnolphe and Agnès, he goes far beyond the two-dimensionality of farce to the three-dimensionality of great drama, in which conflicts take place within the characters themselves and arise from the opposition of various figures rather than from particular situations.

The School for Husbands has classical models (Terence, Boccaccio, and Lope de Vega) from whom Molière takes scenes and dramatic ideas. In addition, he draws on his own experience: Molière was himself a suitor at the time when he wrote the two *Schools*. He then married Armande Béjart, who was twenty years his junior and whose education he himself had supervised. But the autobiographical parallels here, as elsewhere in Molière's work, must be taken with a grain of salt. Sganarelle and Arnolphe are self-portraits only in a very figurative sense; they are projections of the actor rather than of the suitor and husband. Molière was forty years old, the age of the traditional *barbon*—the solid bourgeois graybeard of French comedy. Roles also had to be found for Armande, who had joined the troupe. These are the only facts that we have. Further speculations would be both dangerous and rather unproductive. Contemporary opponents of *The School for Wives* made a great hullaballoo over the personal parallels, but Molière resolutely defended himself. The portraits in the play are objective and distanced, formed in the image of the theater. Their greatness arises from their universal applicability and not from their personal significance.

Sganarelle and Ariste in *The School for Husbands* each have a ward, two orphaned sisters, whom they educate according to their very different concepts and whom they plan to marry. A heated dialogue in the first act establishes the similarities and contrasts between these two temperamentally different brothers. Sganarelle is the strict foster father, a tyrant in his own house, and a patriarchal bourgeois whose hostility to freedom and pleasure borders on misanthropy and hostility to society in general. (In this characteristic, he is a caricatured preliminary study of the misanthropic Alceste.) Ariste is the liberal, stoic man of the world. Molière's first *raisonneur*, he is an advocate for both nature and moderation. He understands education to be the process of finding oneself by mixing with the world at large; it is not the drilling-in of commandments and prohibitions as practiced by Sganarelle. To put it in more general terms, Ariste considers human behavior to be a balancing act between adaptation to the majority (*le plus grande nombre*)—that is, to the society in which one lives— and individual freedom, which is governed equally by instincts, inclinations, and reason. Human conduct is

not a matter of principles and abstractions, as Sganarelle believes, but rather of constant improvisation
dictated by particular circumstances and factors.

Ariste allows his ward to be molded by the flow of
events, to live as a young person among young people;
aware of their difference in age, he does not interfere
with the process himself. Ariste's behavior illustrates
flexibility, moderation, and confidence in reality.
Sganarelle, however, mockingly scorns such behavior.
Certain that he is ten times cleverer than Ariste, he
attempts to mold his ward to suit himself, isolating her
by his social puritanism, and removing her far from
the temptations of the world. He allows her no freedom of choice and no possibility of learning from experience. The audience senses that this attempt must
fail. The dramatist shows how it fails by devising a
plot, constructed of many ironies, in which the action
diverges down separate but symmetrical paths. In her
effort to become herself, Isabella, the girl who has
been anxiously watched over and kept far from external influences, is forced to be a cunning intriguer who
strives to get away from her mentor. Léonore, the girl
who has been freely educated, voluntarily chooses her
mentor as a husband because he has allowed her to
become herself.

The formula is familiar: he who has enjoyed freedom chooses order, whereas he who has been kept in a
state of bondage must procure freedom for himself.
Ariste's tactics are risky, but Sganarelle's are down-
right dangerous. No comedy could be created out of
Ariste's conduct, whereas Sganarelle's behavior is a
comic powder keg. Sganarelle runs blindly into the

trap Isabella sets him in self-defense. No premeditated plan of action is initiated against him. The intrigue develops slowly out of a series of improvised pranks which cause Sganarelle, the prison warden, to open the door of this presumptuously constructed prison and himself become the agent of Isabella's liberation.

In *The School for Wives*, a similar maneuver leads to the denouement, though it is carried out in a psychologically more compelling manner. In *The School for Husbands* the psychological motives are of less importance. As in traditional farce, the protagonist's stupidity and conceit merely serve as the driving force that makes him the butt of the intrigue. Isabella's improvisations are successful because they are derived from her knowledge of Sganarelle's weaknesses. They are dramatic and comic because at each moment of extreme danger Sganarelle's self-righteous blindness allows his victim to escape and thereby come one step closer to her goal.

Valère, a young neighbor, is in love with Isabella and she with him, but they must cultivate this love mutely and from a distance, since they are kept under the Argus-eyed surveillance of Sganarelle. In the end the lovers are united, as is customary in comedy, which snaps its fingers at the old lover because he is an unnatural figure. But the end is reached in a more subtle manner than is customary. The characteristic complexity of this play's intrigue serves a different purpose from that of mere buffoonery; it profiles the stupid protagonist so precisely that he becomes a truly living figure.

Isabella makes Sganarelle into the go-between for

herself and Valère. While leading Sganarelle to believe that Valère's suit is repellent to her, she gives
Valère to understand that she loves him and would
like to become his, if he will only help her to escape
from Sganarelle. The sealed messages, the secret
maneuver in which a letter containing Isabella's un-
ambiguous confession of love is conveyed *to* Valère
by Sganarelle, who believes it to be an unopened letter
from Valère, the double-edged conversations between
Sganarelle and Isabella, between Sganarelle and Valère—these are all classical episodes of comic intrigue.
Similarly classic is the comical crescendo at the end of
the third act, in which Isabella spins a dangerous chain
of lies in order to steal away from Sganarelle's house
and into Valère's. Alleging that her sister Léonore is
involved in a love affair with Valère, Isabella throws
so much sand in Sganarelle's eyes that he believes that
it is Léonore who has left his house and slipped into
the neighbor's house. In reality it is Isabella, but
Sganarelle is so firmly convinced that it is Léonore
that he has a commissioner and a notary quickly
brought to him in order to have the lovers married as
soon as possible. He thinks that in doing this he is
dealing Ariste a blow; but this counteraction actually
serves to give support to the play's main action. In
sending for the notary, Sganarelle only hastens his
own ruin: it is Isabella, the girl who has been kept
discreetly at home, whom he is going to unite in marriage with Valère for better or for worse.

There they stand in front of the house, these two
very different brothers, the one supposedly triumphing by cunning, the other already resigned to the loss

of his ward, the former having through his action contravened all the rules of natural humanity, the latter
with the help of reason having conquered his baser
inclinations. And these two are the only ones who do
not know what is happening. Everyone else, including
the audience, is laughing up his sleeve at Sganarelle,
who could almost be a tragic or a sympathetic figure if
he were not so infinitely conceited and self-righteous.
Up until the end, when the trap has snapped shut
and he has lost everything, the laughter is at his
expense.

Léonore's arrival clears up the intrigue. She—this
gentle antithesis of comedy—is weary of young men
and loves only her Ariste. Though she proves herself
to be the more serious and better educated of the two
sisters, from the point of view of the comedy itself,
she is the far less interesting girl. Ariste's generosity is
rewarded while Sganarelle's pettiness and arrogance
are punished. The punishment is severe indeed, since it
condemns him to isolation! It is as if an inflammable
foreign object had to be removed from a web which it
would otherwise ignite—this web being society itself.

Despite everything that has occurred during the
course of the play, Sganarelle fails to understand why
such things happen to him; indeed, Molière allows
Sganarelle to feel strengthened in his prejudices and
principles by these events. Therefore, the conclusion
is not sad but, in a mildly cruel way, satisfying; Sganarelle has deserved nothing else. Since he is incapable
of learning, it is impossible for him to gain any insight
into his own character and behavior. Therefore, he has
no right to wish to educate others. Long before the

end of the play, Sganarelle's poetic damnation is fore-
shadowed in many of the ironies dispersed throughout
the dialogue. He will have due cause to eat those very
words which he utters in reference to others, but
which really reflect truths concerning himself. Such
words appear like leitmotives throughout the play; for
example, he says to Ariste: "soon we will all laugh"
and to Valère: "poor boy." Again and again he voices
such sentiments, which prove indeed to be true but in
a completely different sense than was meant: "Girls
become what one makes them" or "I see that my les-
sons have taken root in your soul."

Sganarelle, like Ariste, has completed the education
of his ward. In both cases this education proceeds towards the same end: the free choice of a husband, but
in Sganarelle's case *malgré lui*. The ironic reversal in
which Sganarelle is exposed as a blockhead, after having considered himself to be so clever that he could
afford to laugh maliciously at others, is an example of
high comic art. This reversal is high comedy because
it is not grounded merely in the external plot mecha-
nisms of farce but is deeply embedded in the psychol-
ogy of the character himself. Sganarelle thus becomes
a more fully ripened comic figure, nearly entirely liberated from the stiffness of the *commedia dell'arte*
mask and Gallic farce.

The School for Wives could just as well be called
The School for Husbands. The theme and result as
well as the plot's main outlines are the same in this
more mature and more realistic variation. Plot duplications are eliminated and the figures are arranged somewhat differently, but the comic center consisting of

the *barbon* and his comic fate are a repetition of the earlier play. It is as if Molière were not yet finished with this theme. Indeed, much later in *The Learned Women*, he once again dedicates a play to this theme, which also provides the undercurrent of a series of other plays. The first *School* had been a success; the second *School* was a still greater one, which is precisely why it caused a scandal. The agitation by those who envied Molière, as well as by those groups of snobs and religious zealots who felt themselves to have been attacked in this work, was so violent that Molière felt compelled to defend himself. This defense succeeded brilliantly, because most of the public—including the King, the court, and a number of influential persons—sided with him.

For his polemics he chose the medium most suited to him. He wrote two controversial plays designed to present his point of view in the most satisfying manner: *The Critique of The School for Wives* and *The Versailles Impromptu*. The *Critique* was a witty discussion play and the *Impromptu* a description of a rehearsal taking place in his own theater. Both plays fulfilled their mission of silencing Molière's opponents.

The scandal over *The School for Wives* stemmed not so much from its theme as from Molière's dramatic methods. (His opponents—particularly those precious snobs who militantly urged the emancipation of women—were not, after all, reactionary educators.) It was a controversy of pedants against practitioners, snobs against realists—affectation and prudery against candor. *The School for Wives* was a novelty on the stage. With graceful audacity Molière mixed his genres, ignored Aristotelian rules, and launched satirical barbs in all directions.

The comedy is "internalized": the intrigue is only weakly developed; the plot consists of reports and meetings, and most of what happens takes place within the characters themselves, mainly within the two protagonists Arnolphe and Agnès. Molière shows us the inner action in detail. Conversely, the external occurrences spurring internal activity are only sketchily reported on.

Arnolphe—the patriarchal guardian of morality, the vicious slanderer, the obdurate dogmatist—falls into a dilemma which has fatal consequences and robs him of that which he holds dearest just because he does, after all, have a rudimentary sense of honor. He is a friend of Oronte and, therefore, also of Oronte's son, Horace, who eventually steals Agnès from him. Horace—unaware of Arnolphe's relationship to Agnès—chooses him as his confidant and accomplice in his pursuit of Agnès. Arnolphe is thus forced to play along in a game which cuts deeper and deeper into his own flesh. He can at no time break from this position because he is afraid to appear ridiculous and because he would lose his ward if he laid his cards on the table.

In all innocence Horace reports to him the step-by-step progress of his campaign to win Agnès's love. He also asks Arnolphe to advise him on the efficacy of this or that maneuver. Horace then successfully executes the maneuver in defiance of the unknown harem guard who, in reality, is standing right before his eyes. Thus, to the audience's delight Horace informs Arnolphe of all those things which have been plotted against him and carried on behind his back. Arnolphe is therefore totally conversant with everything that is going on and, after learning of each new letter, rendezvous, or plan for abduction and marriage, he takes whatever measures he can to avert the feared disaster. But in doing this, he actually assists in bringing about his ruin all the more quickly and inevitably.

Arnolphe has fate against him in the guise of his own stubborn and intractable nature; accident, however, assists Horace. What the former vainly attempts to achieve through force, namely, Agnès's favor, falls into the lap of the latter of its own accord. Like Sganarelle, Arnolphe has systematically educated his ward in such a way that—in an ironic reversal of his real intentions—he inevitably loses her. But it is "natural" that he lose her. How he loses her in a poetic and marvelous fashion at the end of the play when Agnès's true identity is revealed is an example of poetic parable, not an imitation of life. What really counts, however, is the psychological activity focused on in the course of the play.

Critics have rightly pointed out that *The School for Wives* contains material suitable for a bourgeois tragedy. Arnolphe could be seen as a tragic hero who has had to suffer a loss because his passion has conquered his sense of reality. But Arnolphe is a comic figure because he neither understands nor seeks to understand himself, the society in which he lives, or the instincts and needs of other human beings. It does not occur to him that the innocent and naive girl is in far greater danger precisely because of this innocence

The *Precious Damsels* as produced by the Comédie Française in 1960. It was with this play that Molière began his career as a writer.

Lise Delamare and Georges Descrieres as members of Molière's troupe in a 1959 production of *The Versailles Impromptu* by the Comédie Française.
STUDIO LIPNITZKI

Brian Bedford as ARNOLPHE tries to revive David Dukes as HORACE in the New York production of *The School for Wives* in Richard Wilbur's translation.
VAN WILLIAMS

Louis Jouvet "humbles" himself before DAMIS in his
own production of *Tartuffe*. ORGON sides with the impostor against his own son.
STUDIO LIPNITZKI

Erwin Geschonneck in the title role of the 1954 Berlin
Ensemble production of *Don Juan*. Norbert Christian is
his servant, SGANARELLE.
WILLY SAEGER

FAMOUS FRENCH ACTORS
INTERPRET MOLIÈRE

Left: Charles Dullin as
HARPAGON in *The Miser*

Lower left: Jean-Louis
Barrault as ALCESTE in
The Misanthrope

Lower right: Fernand
Ledoux plays title role in
Tartuffe

Opposite: Louis Jouvet
interprets *Don Juan*
FRENCH CULTURAL EMBASSY

Robert Bazil, right, as DANDIN and Pierre
Mayrand as LUBIN in Roger Planchon's 1961
production of *Georges Dandin*.
PHOTO PIC

derived from her imposed isolation than she would have been had she been allowed to study the customs of the world by living in it. Forbidden to think, she acts from pure, childlike instinct, choosing whatever is pleasant and whatever makes her happy. She follows the "voice of her heart," asserting: "one cannot really wish to drive away what is so very pleasant."

The picture of married life which Arnolphe draws for her "puts her in a bad mood even through its mere description." (The maxims which he has her read aloud are a grand satire on the bourgeois-clerical demands for submissiveness which men make upon their wives.) In her dialogue with Arnolphe (Act IV, Scene 4), she grants him no more than what is due to a strict father; the relationship between Agnès and Arnolphe is basically one of father and daughter. She is even unable to show him gratitude since he has left her in a state of ignorance thanks to his system of education based upon self-interest. How could she share his principles of conduct since these principles have merely been designed to serve his own best interests and, therefore, oppose all of her own needs.

That Arnolphe does not or will not understand Agnès's point of view is comprehensible, for he sees her not as a person but as an object, as a function of his own wishes. But this is dangerous even for him, since she is, after all, a person. She learns this on the hard road of rebellion, of deception, and of a slow awareness of the unnatural position she is in. A father cannot become a husband, or a prison warden a lover. This is the moral which the audience learns, although Arnolphe does not.

It is of no avail that Arnolphe declares his love to
Agnès and that he throws himself at her feet, patheti-
cally discarding the last remnants of his pride, even
promising at the last moment to allow her everything
which he has held back heretofore, if only she will
love him in return. At the extreme edge of his own
existence he meets with extreme resistance; he cannot
change nature. He must come off a loser. In his hands
everything turns into its opposite. Thus the steps
which he undertook in order to avert disaster proved
to be the most stupid thing that he could have done;
they isolated him from Agnès more than they isolated
Agnès from the world. His conceited cleverness becomes the source of the comedy, for it does him no
good. In the simplest possible manner he is outwitted
by Agnès's innocence and Horace's worldliness, although, or perhaps precisely because, he has been
given such exact information as to what is going on.
Once again the comic character is brought to ruin
because he lacks the ability to adapt himself, because
he lacks the skill to improvise, and because he lacks
insight into the nature of the rules by which the game
of life is played.

The basic comic situation gives rise to a whole series
of funny secondary situations. The two simple-
minded servants engaged in Arnolphe's behalf are
more a hindrance than a help because of their inade-
quacy. They bring about the decisive delays which
help Horace to success in his maneuvers.

The comic language Molière has put into Arnolphe's mouth has a similar function. As Horace's
fatherly friend, he must hold his tongue against his

will and say the opposite of what he would really like to say; often he is actually driven to speechlessness, because it is only in this way that he can keep his secret and avoid appearing ridiculous. The "oufs" and "ohs"—which are disguised as coughs (Molière's coughs) and which in reality give expression to his soul's torment and his impotence—are communicated to the audience as a grotesque form of ambiguity. The quadruply repeated "Ohs" of Arnolphe's final exit express anger, dismay, and pain as well as the inarticulateness typical of the injured dupe whose carefully constructed world has collapsed. They speak volumes. At other times Arnolphe was well able to make speeches. Feeling himself to be superior, he indulged in torrents of arguments, proverbs, and bourgeois wisdom. With great fluency he was able to contradict Chrysalde's worldly philosophy of life and to lecture Agnès. However, as soon as this feeling of superiority began to crumble, speech also failed him. When Agnès rejects him and he realizes that he loves her more than he values his doctrines and his reputation, he begins to stutter. When he loses her he can only say "Oh."

Tartuffe
(Le Tartuffe, ou L'Imposteur, 1664–69)

Whether art can change men is debatable. It is certain, however, that Molière's art at least deeply perplexed the people of his own age. The many scandals that surrounded his plays and the many interdictions that were imposed upon them speak eloquently on this point. Most telling of all was the five-year battle over *Tartuffe*. The controversy indicated that with this play Molière had stepped into a wasp's nest and had either wittingly or unwittingly violated various taboos. It could have cost him his career if he had not had the tacit confidence of the King as well as of a series of influential and like-minded men and if he himself had not been possessed of unique endurance and a diplomat's skill at maneuvering.

His theater was provocative, although it is difficult to say whether his plays changed men, whether after an evening at *Tartuffe* hypocrites beat their breasts and decided to become men of honor, whether bigots were converted to true faith, or whether the tyrannical fathers of families henceforth expressed a more forebearing kind of love. What we do know, however, is that many considered themselves to have been directly attacked in this work. Such people sensed that their life style had been put into jeopardy. Moreover, they felt threatened by the laughter and mockery this play aimed at hypocrisy and bigotry in particular and —implicitly—at the church and religiosity in general.

The attacks against Molière carried on by the so-called *Cabal* (led by Molière's former school friend the Prince de Conti), by a group of religious zealots who were fairly influential at court, by a series of prominent clergymen, and, above all, by the militant anti-reformation Society of the Holy Sacrament terrified even the King and forced him to issue his first interdiction against the play. The second one was handed down a few months later by the president of the Parisian Parliament, in spite of string-pulling by Molière and his friends. A third interdiction followed from the Archbishop of Paris. In other words, the highest secular and temporal powers considered *Tartuffe* to be a very dangerous matter, a revolutionary document which could arouse in the Parisian theatergoers revolutionary thoughts against both the state and religion, thereby endangering the established order.

The controversy did not so much create the tensions as bring to light a situation which had long existed. As a result, insults which the religious zealots had intended for the liberals (the so-called *libertins*—freethinkers and anticlerics) and which the liberals had intended for the zealots, were all heaped upon the head of *Tartuffe*'s unfortunate author. It is possible that the play was partly responsible for the fact that the Society of the Holy Sacrament was dissolved after the death of the Queen Mother.

We do not know what Molière's real purpose was, but we do know at least this: by means of this play he wanted to deal a blow to those people who had been hostile to him from the very beginning of his years in Paris. In the preface to the printed edition of *Tartuffe*, he once again affirms the thesis put forth in *The Precious Damsels* that comedy should portray the ridiculous and false representatives of otherwise honorable behavior and that its function is *de corriger les vices des hommes* (to correct the vices of men) by exposing deceit, excesses of all kinds, and lack of honor.

But in *Tartuffe* no true Christian appears at the side of the pious impostor. The honest character is once again, as in both *Schools*, the *raisonneur* who is on the side of the *juste milieu*. Cléante is the *honnête homme* who defends not so much true religion as true humanity, proclaiming common sense and not faith. The arrangement of characters in Molière's comedy does not involve a contrast between one or two comic (ridiculous or vicious) figures and a group of normal people whose spokesman preaches moderation and sociability. The *raisonneur* is not the active opponent of the main figures but rather the moderator between contradictory positions. Moreover, as modern criticism has unanimously established, the *raisonneur* is certainly not the voice of the author's own philosophy but rather a dramatic corrective whose function it is to create poetic symmetry in the play. Thus Cléante is not Tartuffe's opponent and only in a limited sense Orgon's (in respect to his attitude toward society). There are no mirror images; Molière has left his personal opinions on religion out of the play. He only comments upon *certain* of religion's representatives, but he does so in such a way that *all* contemporary representatives of religion felt attacked.

Tartuffe is not concerned with man's relationship to God, but with man's relationship to man. The position of Tartuffe and Orgon with respect to their God, to Christian dogma, and to religion in general is not a point of discussion. Of the essence is, however, how they relate to the human beings in their dramatic environment; their hypocrisy and bigotry have a profound and negative effect upon these people, and it is with this that the play is concerned.

It is generally agreed that *Tartuffe* is one of Molière's masterpieces and a masterpiece of European comedy. How and why this is so is more difficult to establish. There are innumerable theories concerning the nature of the comic elements in this play, the significance of its title figure, possible models taken from real life, the artificial or ingenious solution with which the play concludes, the various versions, and finally, the possibility that *Tartuffe* is a tragi-comedy or even a tragedy if the last act or the last two are left out. *Tartuffe* is the ultimate play and provides the ultimate role for every ambitious French actor, just as *Hamlet* does for the English actor and *Faust* does for the German actor. There will always be new Tartuffes. Every age has its own Tartuffe and its own forms of hypocrisy.

Our admiration for this play is kindled first of all by its perfect form, by the graceful curve the five-act plot describes from its constricted introduction through the almost unbearable dramatic climaxes in the third and fourth acts to the surprise-laden prestissimo of the denouement the play is a triumph of poetic organization. Despite an astonishingly meager plot, how the relationships between the figures constantly shift! Because of his skill in maneuvering the others, Tartuffe, who is absent from the stage more often than he is present, nevertheless stands at the helm of affairs until the very last moment.

In this play we are once again superficially concerned with an arranged and unnatural marriage. Orgon wishes to wed his young daughter to his friend Tartuffe rather than to the man she loves and to whom she has already been promised. The action is further concerned with the disinheriting of a natural heir in favor of an impostor, who has slipped inside the family circle and disunited it. Finally, *Tartuffe* directs itself to undermining the absolute rule of the bourgeois *pater familias*. The disrupted order to be restored at the end of the comedy is the order of the family, which has been disturbed in two ways: from outside, by the impostor Tartuffe, who like a cuckoo has settled himself more and more securely into another's nest, and from within its core, by the father's abuse of his authority. As in many other plays by Molière, the central comic figure is once again the conceited bourgeois whose religiosity and bigotry are exploited for quite worldly purposes.

Orgon's foolishness and his excesses are cured when

the impostor is outwitted. However, he immediately falls into another just as "bourgeois" excess; he goes from bondage to blind rage, and both these excesses hurt his family. From the point of view of the comedy, it is not Tartuffe who is the real protagonist, but Orgon. His infatuation with Tartuffe—which initiates (or intensifies) the bigotry which causes him to betray his family's interests—is the madness which must be comically illuminated. Orgon does not know what he is doing, for his will has been crippled by his madness. His conceit cannot be shattered by reasonable persuasion but only by the drastic measures his family undertakes.

Tartuffe, on the other hand, always has control of himself. He calculates, manipulates, and plays his various roles with the brilliance and detachment of a great actor; will has control. His actions are sometimes comic, for example, when he sanctimoniously insists that the maid Dorine cover her bosom, or when he admits to Orgon's wife, Elmire, that his adulterous love is an uncontrollable, human, all-too-human passion natural in a pious man. However, he is usually sinister—a threat rather than a ridiculous dramatic character (a French Iago?). And yet, in his preface, Molière himself has characterized Tartuffe as the protagonist of his play and has designated his vices (hypocrisy, sanctimoniousness, and ruthless fraudulence) as the objects of the satire. Orgon is not a sanctimonious hypocrite, he is an obsessed man. Tartuffe, on the other hand, wears masks which he drops and changes as the situation requires. As a masquerader who is exposed, he is a figure of comedy. But in the

most serious sense, he is not comic and laughable but
grotesque and macabre, an altogether terrifying figure.

Le Tartuffe, ou L'Imposteur (Tartuffe or The Impostor) was the title Molière gave to his last version
of this play, which was preceded by several others
that have been lost and cannot be reconstructed. In a
milder version, written after the first *Tartuffe* had
been suppressed, Molière has Tartuffe remove his
black coat with its white clerical collar and don the
worldly costume of a nobleman, complete with riding
whip. He attempted in this way to make it clear that
he was not accusing the church as a whole of hypocrisy; instead, he was taking aim either at the pseudo-
Christian layman, or simply at an ambitious, impecu-
nious, but clever young man who, like Stendhal's
Julien Sorel, meant to make his way to the top of
society and would shrink at nothing in this pursuit.
The appositive "impostor" in the title turns one's at-
tention away from the religious aspect of Tartuffe and
characterizes the external course of the comedy's action.

Under false pretenses, Tartuffe has insinuated himself into Orgon's family and into the master's confidence. He has established himself there like a drone,
alienating Orgon from his wife and children. Though
he has been promised the daughter's hand in marriage,
he makes an indecent proposal to Orgon's wife, and
then shamelessly denies this when Damis, Orgon's son,
confronts him with this in the presence of his father.
He manipulates Orgon to such an extent that the latter
drives his own son from the house and disinherits him

in Tartuffe's favor, cleaving ever more fanatically to his idol.

The "worldly" members of Orgon's family have long ago seen through the impostor and try to catch him out. They arrange a second tête-à-tête between Tartuffe and Madame Elmire during which Orgon, concealed under a table, is witness to Tartuffe's un-ambiguous proposals. Orgon finally breaks out of the hypnotic magic circle at this point. Tartuffe once again tries to ingratiate himself, but when this fails he lets his mask of friendship fall. He gives Orgon to understand that he has himself provided him with the means to destroy him and his entire family. In a mo-ment of confidence, Orgon has thoughtlessly allowed to fall into Tartuffe's hands a strongbox containing papers and documents hostile to the monarchy. This box had been entrusted to Orgon's safekeeping by a friend now in exile. Tartuffe declares his intention of denouncing Orgon before the King, asserting that he will take action immediately. Since in making Tartuffe his sole heir, Orgon has also signed over his house, the impostor makes preparations to evict the family from these premises. He triumphantly returns from having carried out his act of denunciation in order to super-vise the eviction personally. However, at the moment of greatest danger to the family, a messenger from the King arrives and arrests Tartuffe instead of Orgon—a miraculous end!

In the past, Tartuffe had committed a number of serious frauds. The King had only allowed him to hold sway in Orgon's house in order to catch him in a new act of deception. Orgon goes unpunished because of his former services on behalf of the state. He and his family have gotten away with only a bad scare. The daughter Mariane gets her lover Valère, Elmire's virtue remains irreproachable, Orgon and his mother, Madame Pernelle, are cured of their bigotry and their Tartuffe-craze. The impostor is brought to ruin, but only through intervention from outside, through the affixing of a happy end.

The actual substance of this play is to be found in a subtle and complex "inner" plot which runs parallel to the simple external action. While the latter is kept in motion by the active villain and only concerns the passive victim of the fraud secondarily, the inner action concerns all the characters because it deals with the fundamental questions of power relationships and proper social behavior in general: rightful love, Eros and Agape, moderation and excess, deception and sincerity. Molière leaves unanswered the question as to whether Tartuffe and Orgon are perhaps true believers after all, despite the fact that their behavior has destroyed the equilibrium of the family. He is concerned only with the evil consequences of their exaggerated religiosity and their unnatural relationship with each other. (In many modern performances of this play, Orgon's latent homosexuality is intimated.)

Orgon's excess consists of the fact that under Tartuffe's influence he completely puts aside the interests of his own family to force his daughter into a marriage against her will—and in opposition to his own original pledge—and to disinherit his son. He does not even defend his wife's virtue. This naturally implies a concealed criticism of the Christian precept that one should leave father and mother and follow Christ. It also implies a criticism of Christianity in general, which gives more importance to man's relationship to God than to his relationship with other human beings. But Molière protects himself by ascribing a completely unchristian attitude to the man giving orders to Orgon. Tartuffe is not just a Pharisee who gives the external appearance of righteousness. (Pharisaism is the first thing stressed in Tartuffe's initial appearance, Act III, Scene 2, which is delayed in order to heighten the tension of the play. Tartuffe begins by ordering his servant to put away his hair shirt and his scourge, and then he puritanically demands that Dorine cover her bosom.) Tartuffe also breaks—or at least intends to break—more than one of the ten commandments. His attempted seduction of Elmire, his desire for Orgon's possessions, and his general lack of love for his fellow man all reveal Tartuffe's lack of Christian spirit.

What the family reproaches him with, however, is not his unchristian nature but his total lack of social feeling: they, whose interests are in jeopardy, recognize that behind Tartuffe's hypocritical piety lies crass egotism. Tartuffe has taken their father from them by making Orgon completely subordinate to him; he plans to take their stepmother as well—in addition the sister, the house, and the family's possessions. Their dislike is directed against the swindler who, under the cloak of humility and modesty, criticizes their "worldly" way of life while himself indulging in far more offensive conduct. It is thus his falseness and his interference which they oppose, for they have recognized Tartuffe's worldly motives. Only their father and Madame Pernelle remain blind. Tartuffe hypnotizes those who are foolish and conceited; those who are reasonable and practical (Elmire, Cléante, the maid Dorine) are immune to him.

At the core of the play is the triangle consisting of Orgon-Elmire-Tartuffe; the other characters are peripheral to this configuration. Orgon's relationship to Tartuffe determines his relationship to Elmire (negatively); Tartuffe's relationship to Elmire damages and destroys his relationship to Orgon; Elmire's fidelity to Orgon causes the hypocrite to appear in his true light, as an impostor. Tartuffe's relationship to Elmire is Janus-headed: publicly, he criticizes her natural worldliness, her guests and her pleasures; privately, he wishes to have her in his power as he wishes for the possession of all of Orgon's other goods. Since the mask of piety does not enchant her, he puts on the mask of the passionate lover. (Tartuffe should not be played as a dessicated, elderly man of the cloth. From the very beginning he must be shown as impressively masculine, since his appearance is repeatedly praised throughout the play. The self-confidence with which he goes about an act of seduction must be rooted in his awareness of his considerable physical attraction.)

The short scene with Dorine and the neckerchief is a dramatic prelude to the seduction. Molière is not only satirizing the puritan whose thoughts are constantly on sin, he is also characterizing his Tartuffe as a man suffering from sexual frustration. In this way, he gives his audience a clue to the dramatic developments

that follow. Dorine sees through Tartuffe as she sees
through everyone. Elmire, the person most affected
by his behavior, also sees through him. After she has
recovered from the surprise his unexpected immoral
proposition has caused her, she decides with the sure
instinct of a woman that the external appearance of
virtue is not as important as outwitting the impostor.
In the second tête-à-tête, she meets the hypocrite
with hypocrisy and lures from him his most com-
promising words: "Yes, one is pious, but one is also
human . . ./you are surprised that a man like me can
speak like this?/But what am I to do? I am not an
angel."

The fresh air of farce enters the comedy with
Dorine. With the earthy lack of respect and shrewd
independence of a child of the people, she gives a
piece of her mind to Tartuffe, to Orgon, and to the
young lovers who begin to mistrust one another as
Orgon's wicked commands enmesh them. Moliére's
best comic scenes are built around Dorine. In gesture
and in speech, she plays the *provocatrice* in a provocative play, and most gloriously in her scenes with
Orgon. This begins with his first entrance, the famous
dialogue in which the Orgon interrupts Dorine's reports concerning Madame Elmire's illness during his
absence with a monotonous repetition of questions
concerning Tartuffe's well-being. Elmire has this ail-
ment, says Dorine; "And Tartuffe?," he responds.
Tartuffe is greedy, egotistical, and unbearable, says
Dorine (the only one who dares to say these things so
plainly). "*Le pauvre homme*" (the poor man), says
Orgon.

Dorine stands for loyalty to the family, the rights of youth, and the rights of women. When Orgon peremptorily confronts Mariane with his plans for her marriage to Tartuffe, it is not Mariane who protests, but Dorine; it is she who upbraids him with his tyranny in his own house, his weakness and lack of fatherly behavior. She boldly interrupts him and ignores his brusque commands to shut up. She effects a reconciliation between the two lovers who have quarreled in a choreographically planned scene laden with misunderstandings and coquettry. Her sense of reality triumphs over all of the irrational rules of the social game. Thus she becomes the active ally of the passive *raisonneur*, an outsider who ties up loose ends and undoes masks. As we will see later in *The Would-Be Gentleman*, the maid and her mistress make common cause: while each employs different social methods, they fight together against the fancies and deceits which jeopardize their small, solid world.

Don Juan
(Don Juan, ou Le Festin de Pierre, 1665)

Molière's version of the Spanish legend, which like so much other Spanish material made its way to France by way of Italy in the seventeenth century, is today considered one of a trio of his masterpieces completed by *Tartuffe* and *The Misanthrope*. This is not merely because the play was written, as were the two others, during those years in which Molière's comic art had mastered the genre. Nor is it because like them *Don Juan* was provocative to both the state and audiences. The play is a masterpiece equal to the two others because of the dramatist's cheerful and subtle embodiment of the eternally human figure of the seducer, the individualist who challenges both society and authority. Because Molière's Don Juan is such a multifaceted figure, we are presented with characters who represent a wide spectrum of problems and themes.

And yet *Don Juan* was written with Molière's left hand, metaphorically speaking; that is, it was written in great haste and in prose, because a quick substitute for the suppressed *Tartuffe* had to be found. A plot was available which was familiar to the public in all of its details and characters. Moreover, this public had already enthusiastically received other versions of the story and thus the theme was fashionable. To profit from this situation, Molière added some specifically French elements to the traditional material at hand. It was easy to spot many parallels between the characters in *Don Juan* and personalities at court. The play also revealed a further development of patterns originating in *Tartuffe*. For example, Molière's protagonist plays one extra role not assumed by the Spanish Don Juan of Tirso de Molina or other Don Juans: just before his destiny overtakes him, he turns hypocrite. People surmised that this Don Juan was a lightly disguised portrait of the erstwhile roué, the Prince de Conti, who had become a principal member of the Society of the Holy Sacrament after his spectacular religious conversion.

Once again there was a scandal and short-lived success. Molière was compelled to make cuts. The play appeared fifteen times on the stage of the Palais Royal and then disappeared from the billboards. Was this because of royal intervention? Or caution? Or the result of a fear that this new attack upon religious zealots would ruin his chances of resurrecting *Tartuffe*? We do not know Molière's reasons for withdrawing *Don Juan*.

Molière never revived the play and did not even publish it himself. (In 1682, a "mild" version appeared in the *Oeuvres complètes*, but it was some time before the original version was again made accessible to readers.) Some time later, others indulged in heated polemics on this play; then it was completely forgotten. It was only recently restored to the repertoire, and it is now admiringly called a "masterpiece."

In Molière's total work, *Don Juan* is a play *sui generis*. One cannot find in it even a trace of the classical rules that in his other plays were at least used as a guide (if not as a constricting framework). The play also raised considerable doubts about a fourth classical dramatic unity; the unified conception of the title figure. The irregularity of the action in this play is practically Elizabethan. The loosely connected episodes, quick changes of locale, and vagueness of time give the play a picaresque structure held together by the figure of Don Juan himself, represented in every scene either through his own appearance or that of his mirror image, the servant Sganarelle.

Don Juan contains two explicit forces in opposition: Don Juan himself and the world of the others; Sganarelle comically mediates between these in his role as both the ironic provocateur's opposite and his principal confidant, assistant, and most insightful commentator. In other words, society is placed in opposition to the individualist whose mediary is once again the timid, comically awkward servant. Molière fashions his play by combining sections, rather than by developing it causally. He can assume that the audience knows the legendary story, and that the main figures, the course of action, and the play's conclusion are familiar.

Molière's version is a play of encounters, each of

which reveals another aspect of Don Juan, and in each of which he assumes a different role. His repertoire is rich and primarily concerns three areas of life and ways of coping with them: eroticism, or the relationship between men and women; metaphysics, or man's relationship to religion; and respectability, or man's relationship to his family and to the world in which he lives. That Don Juan is an actor (though in a different manner from Tartuffe, who never allows the mask that has become his second nature to drop) can be seen in the detachment with which he pursues everything. Don Juan remains the same whether he is seducing women, challenging noblemen preoccupied with their honor (his father, the jilted Elvire's brothers, even the statue of the Commander), or behaving blasphemously.

Don Juan's characteristic gesture is his attitude of opposition. A man who relativizes everything, he is a skeptic and sufficient unto himself. Don Juan holds firmly to his "libertine" philosophy, which is designed for the asocial individual, and not as an ethic for everyone to live by. His libertinism represents a philosophy of self-satisfaction which knows no scruple with regard to conventions, and shows no concern for the wishes and feelings of others, who only exist as objects for him. It is a philosophy of living life moment by moment without concern for past or future, a philosophy in which the individual derives pleasure from his superiority over other human beings, whether this superiority is demonstrated in games of love, in verbal dispute, or in the skillful exposure of his opponent's weaknesses. Only two figures in the play are equal to Don Juan: the beggar whom he meets on the way to town and (in keeping with the legend) the stone statue of the Commander; the one is a social outsider and the other a supernatural, or rather, a purely theatrical figure. Otherwise there is no one.

Did Molière take Don Juan's side by establishing a configuration so unequally weighted in favor of him? Did mere convention compel him to include the terrifying end in his plans? This can hardly be the case. Would a dramatist identify himself with and give his approval to an excessively self-centered character in one play while in his other plays he consistently condemned promiscuity, extreme individualism, and socially destructive excesses in the most bitterly satiric terms?

Contemporaries enraged by the play accused him of taking sides, but they might as well have accused him of siding with Tartuffe, Harpagon, or Argan. With the protean objectivity peculiar to writers of comedy, the dramatist Molière simultaneously resides both inside and outside of his characters. Don Juan is no more engaging than the other comic heroes of Molière's comedies; he is at most more intelligent. As the exemplification of a particular perspective on life, Don Juan's behavior is portrayed with understanding but without much endeavor to defend him. However, Molière does construct a corrective, albeit a comic one, by allowing the Don's actions and thoughts to be continually reflected in Sganarelle's reactions and comments. While no opposing point of view is produced in this way, the comical refraction creates distance and thus presents a less subjective criticism of Don Juan's views.

The relationship between Don Juan and Sganarelle rests upon an ancient tradition in comedy. Dramatists from Aristophanes to Brecht have employed many variations of the master-servant relationship—itself an essentially human configuration of imbalance—to establish contrasts between high and low comedy. Molière's unequal couple is one of the classical examples of this basic situation of comedy. The servant rather than the master is the real comic center of this play. Don Juan himself only once lands in a truly comical situation. This occurs at the end of the play when the power he has mockingly and defiantly challenged—because he does not believe in things metaphysical—consumes him amid theatrical thunder and lightning.

This end is comical and not tragic as in the case of Doctor Faustus, because Juan has not engaged our sympathy through either repentance or fear. Unconverted and unconvertible, he becomes the victim of his own philosophy. Not a man but a stone breaks his audacity and his hybris. This is comical, fantastic, and theatrical. Moreover, Sganarelle's final words are not devoted to his master but to the loss of his wages; this extinguishes any possible compassion in us and turns it into laughter. Juan may have successfully fulfilled himself while he was still alive, but his fate also shows us the limits of his philosophy of life: no one weeps for him, not even his servant.

Despite his considerable limitations as a thinker, Sganarelle, the timid and superstitious philosopher has enough native wit to understand and to describe Don Juan. (His fault is the reverse of Juan's, for he believes nearly everything, while Juan believes almost nothing.) He watches or helps Juan carry out his escapades with a mixture of admiration and disapproval. For his part, he lacks the courage, as well as the material and spiritual freedom, to imitate his master; however, as Don Juan's servant he vicariously experiences a good deal. This helps to reinforce his primitive fear of God. Though in his master's presence his criticism of Juan must often hide behind transparently forced approval, he constantly notes that "the anger of heaven will strike the master one of these days."

This judgment reveals that Molière has bestowed upon the stupid Sganarelle a depth of insight which surpasses that of the clever Don Juan. After every new difficulty stemming from Don Juan's adventures, Sganarelle complains of his lot of having to serve a *seigneur méchant homme* (a wicked master); for as the paid, if unwilling servant, he must also face the music for his master's deeds. He serves this master not because he feels it his duty to do so, nor because he zealously desires to convert him, nor because he is particularly devoted to him. Sganarelle serves Don Juan for the sake of his wages, for mere financial gain. The comedy realistically presents the material motives of human beings, and also the fact that these motives often cross and contradict each other. In the end, Sganarelle is cheated of his wages because, in his stupidity, he has served a false master.

Sganarelle's discourse, which reveals his preference for long, proverb-ridden speech spiced with *patois*, provides a continuous contrabass in the complex orchestration of the play's musical score. This contrabass repeats, echoes, and often bowdlerizes those things which Don Juan has taught his servant. Nevertheless, the servant instinctively arrives at a deeper level of understanding. Familiar with the motives of the *épouseur à toutes mains* (the irrepressible marrier), Sganarelle is unimpressed by that famous list of women whom Don Juan has "married"; he quickly disposes of it as "a chapter that would take until evening to reel off." He hits the nail on the head when he says to Don Juan: "I know your heart to be the greatest *coureur du monde*" (rover in the world). When he adds: "*vous avez raison, si vous le voulez, mais si vous ne le vouliez pas, ce serait peut-être une autre affaire. . . .*" (You are right if you insist, but if you were not to insist, I might think otherwise . . . Act I, Scene 2), Sganarelle is speaking for himself, from his own convictions.

But just as frequently he must speak against his own convictions. This is true, for example, when he speaks to the two peasant girls Charlotte and Mathurine. Don Juan has made a separate promise of marriage to each of these girls, for this is the method he employs in order to reach his goal in games of love: he makes use of convention and then contravenes it in an ironic manner. Because of this, Sganarelle is compelled to present two conflicting opinions to Charlotte and Mathurine. First, he offers his own real opinion: "Don Juan is a knave; he is ready to marry the whole human race!" He then stiffly and firmly maintains the opposite. Sganarelle's duplicity leads to situations of low comedy in the play. The mask often covers only half of his face, the half belonging to a dependent human being who must continually adapt himself.

When Don Juan holds a golden coin before the beggar's eyes and promises it to him if he will first blaspheme, Sganarelle gives him the following advice: "Go on and swear a little, it can do no harm." This is precisely Sganarelle's own attitude toward life; nothing done in small quantity is harmful. In one conversation with Don Juan, he takes heart and tries to warn his master and to convert him to true faith. This conversation contains that wonderful long speech full of peasant wisdom (Act V, Scene 2); in attempting to present his own philosophy, Sganarelle offers more in the way of zealous enthusiasm than sensible content. On another occasion (Act III, Scene 2), he stumbles over himself during his long, absurd reasoning and literally falls on his nose.

"Your reasoning has fallen on its face," mocks Don Juan. Nevertheless, it is only with Sganarelle that Juan allows himself to be human and friendly, albeit with ironic condescension, and it is only with Sganarelle that he lays aside his masks. He does this not so much because he is dependent upon his servant, as masters frequently are, or because he enjoys frightening Sganarelle. He does so because the play requires that he somewhere explain himself. Molière shows Don Juan not only in action but also as he philosophizes. Sganarelle serves as a good foil to this end, a confidant who has also presumed to think for himself and in whose comically confused head Juan's theories are refracted to a point where they become absurd.

Sganarelle represents a man of total instinct interspersed with peasant shrewdness and superstition. Conversely, Don Juan represents controlled intelligence. His chief impulse is the kind of self-realization achieved by trifling with others in order to control and destroy them. In this pursuit, his chief targets are the female body and male concepts of honor. This impulse, however, is not Faustian, since Don Juan does not strive for knowledge and his philosophizing proceeds no further than skepticism. (His affirmation of the results of arithmetic—"I believe that two times two is four and two times four is eight"—is a pretty thin affair.) Nor does he strive for experience for the sake of better understanding. The relativism with which he approaches sexual morality, aristocratic ethics, and religion has no revolutionary fire in it: his is basically a pleasure in creating confusion and swindling others. Every woman is a challenge for conquest, every man a rival who must be seized by the neck of his own weaknesses—conceit or stupidity—and broken.

Juan does not care about the methods he employs. He promises a woman marriage and everlasting fidelity, although he merely wants her body temporarily. He lives dangerously, not because he has something to defend but because he is a restless spirit who hates boredom. He knows neither fear, nor respect, nor love, nor, indeed, imagination. His Self in the present moment is everything. Because he believes in nothing, he can, if it suits his purposes, act as if he believes in whatever is held sacred by the person with whom he is currently embroiled. With women, he claims to hold

love sacred, although he wants only sex and the pleasure. With aristocrats and burghers, he upholds the
rules of chivalry, which he then ironically employs to
undermine these men.

There is much talk of *honneur* in the play. Molière
embodies this concept in four of the characters: one
woman and three men. First, there is Elvire, whom
Don Juan had snatched from a convent, married, and
then abandoned. Humbled in pride and humiliated in
the eyes of the world, she searches everywhere for
him. She successively appeals to all the conventional
moral and human obligations to which Don Juan is
indifferent: compassion, honor, fidelity, duty, respect
for religion, and fear of divine retribution.

Elvire plays a different role in each of her scenes:
the jealous wife, the religious zealot who has turned
from the world, the selfless lover—all illusions and
conventional postures which barely conceal her con-
suming physical passion and emotional dependence.
Elvire is Don Juan's opposite. She is oriented toward
permanence and exclusiveness, while he has given himself over to the moment and to change. Elvire lives in
a state of continual discord between strictures (social
or religious) and passion (physical or emotional). Juan
rejects the one and atomizes the other by dividing his
passion among countless women. He cannot allow Elvire, or any other woman—indeed, any human being
at all—to possess him or affect him emotionally for
any length of time.

Juan's most human impulses are towards anonymous
people, for example, the beggar who will not sell his
soul for a *louis d'or*. In the end, Juan gives the beggar

the golden coin, not for the sake of God, but—once again ironically—because he loves humanity. He respects in the beggar a strength of will equal to his own, though it operates in a man whose principles are entirely different from his. In another situation, while escaping from the two peasant girls who are beginning to oppress him, Juan comes to an open field where he finds Don Carlos, Elvire's brother, engaged in an uneven struggle with two bandits. Unaware of Carlos's true identity, Juan rescues him. However, as soon as any man or woman becomes a name to him, an identity, or a representative of social responsibility, Don Juan's ironic and destructive urge is once again set in motion.

Now we come to the three masculine concepts of honor represented in this play. First, there is Don Alonso's rigid demand of "an eye for an eye," which serves as an abstract justification for a brutal and primitive nature. Second, there is Don Carlos's attempt to compromise with society. His concept of honor is doubly burdened by the fact that his duty towards his sister conflicts with his duty to Don Juan, who has saved his life. Finally, there is that third conception of honor preached by Don Juan's father, Don Louis, who equates honor with merit. Don Louis condemns his son's life style because it frivolously exploits both Juan's social rank and the names of his ancestors. In Don Louis's view, Don Juan's conduct is incommensurate with his background both in form and in content. All of these three men have become imprisoned in meaningless social postures which they now represent in different degrees of militancy and complexity according to their particular character and age.

These characters all speak a language rich in abstraction, which parodies the *style élevé* (elevated style) of Corneille, just as their attitudes parody those of his characters. In a Corneille tragedy they would appear as heroic figures whose gestures corresponded to social reality. In Molière's comedy, they have become ridiculous reactionaries who confront the immoralist with automatic responses. Not one of them can shake or weaken Don Juan's negativistic point of view. Juan's appeal to the sovereignty of the self, to his own needs and desires, is constantly vindicated, as he confronts each of the individual social types in his environment: the bourgeois (Monsieur Dimanche, the creditor), the peasant (Pierrot, Charlotte, Mathurine), and the aristocrat (Don Alonso, Don Carlos, Don Louis, and Elvire). None of these representatives of their class prevails when confronted with Don Juan's self-affirmation. Something supernatural must intervene to prevent ultimate chaos and the victory of relativism.

It would appear as though Molière, inspired by the legend, threw overboard all precepts concerning the necessity of social conventions. The play provides no contrasting portrait of a society whose proper functioning is essential; therefore, there is also no *raisonneur* who represents the *juste milieu*. The concept of love—which in all of Molière's other plays approve the pairing off of people of the same age and temperament, affirms an equilibrium between the physical and the spiritual impulses, and conceives of the marriage bond as something permanent—is absent from *Don Juan*. The pastoral episode with the peasant girls advocates promiscuity; Elvire's complaints are not characterized as being "natural," and generally speaking hedonism triumphs.

This play gives the lie to those who call Molière a moralist. In it he is primarily concerned with demonstrating a point of view objectively and presenting a dramatic portrait of a hedonist. Only secondarily does he continue a satirical portrait of contemporary morality. Even Don Juan's terrible end represents not a moral but a poetic judgment.

Shortly before his end, Molière's protagonist essays a new role, that of the hypocrite. However, this is nothing but another game designed to confuse others, a momentary whim like everything that Don Juan does, for he has no human core. He is an inversion of Molière's typical contemporary and is, therefore, a spirit who always negates and thus exposes the decayed, outmoded, petrified conventions of ordinary morality. Don Juan himself is deceived only once, but once and for all: while observing the Commander's tomb, he mockingly challenges the statue to move, and it complies. But Juan then disregards the evidence of his eyes and counters it with reason, asserting that "it cannot move." Accepting Don Juan's mocking invitation, the statue comes to dinner. Appearances are affirmed, reason and irony are defeated.

But, of course, this is only a play, and we are only in a theater. Molière wished to bring his play to a conclusion. To do so, he employed the traditional end, but only for poetic and not for moral considerations. In essence, no one has been able to refute Molière's Don Juan convincingly, and it was for this reason that the playwright appeared so dangerous to his contemporaries.

The Misanthrope
(Le Misanthrope, 1664–66)

Among the plays which Molière wrote for the court is an early one entitled *Les Fâcheux* (The Bores). Its theme, developed by means of ballet-comedy—a form which Molière himself invented—is important either as a primary or secondary theme in many of his other plays: how people with different attitudes toward life get on each other's nerves consciously or unwittingly. A character's impatience with the weaknesses of others is one of the chief sources of the play's comedy, but this is in turn counterbalanced by the consistent reaffirmation of the converse position—tolerance and a conciliatory spirit. The protagonists are all people who are unable to compromise with existing social and human realities, people who cannot adapt themselves or change, and who therefore come to grief. Sometimes Molière shows us this intractability in a positive light. But generally man's inability to compromise is presented as being one of

114

those ridiculous inherent difficulties of life which cannot be resolved but only accepted.

For centuries, there has been much discussion about
whether or not Molière himself suffered from this
difficulty, as many signs would seem to indicate. Although he was described by his contemporaries as
being a very sociable and friendly man, great impatience can be read between the lines of his plays and in
their tempo. Indeed, one can see this impatience most
clearly in *The Misanthrope*, in which the protagonist's
irritation with the behavior of his fellow men causes
him to give offense everywhere, to quarrel with each
of his friends in turn, until at the very end he is entirely isolated.

Alceste is, if one cares to put it this way, the most
likable and magnanimous of Moliere's comic heroes,
although it is doubtful that we can really call him a
"comic" character and that this play without a happy
end can be designated as a comedy. If the answer is
"yes," then the play is Molière's most bitter and most
pessimistic comedy, a quasi-Swiftian satire in which, if
we laugh at all, we laugh at a man who wants to be
honorable, charitable, and just, but who cannot get on
with a society which he finds to be fawning, vain,
coquettish, and deceitful. Therefore, we are laughing
at a frustrated idealist who does, indeed, have a specific mania, but a noble and praiseworthy one.
Through our laughter we admit that the protagonist's
ideals are only dreams and will remain only dreams in
a world different from the idealist's dream. In other
words, we admit that reason, according to which

Alceste wishes to live, cannot be employed as the basic principle of human behavior.

Molière played the role of Alceste himself, and since it has been established that he always reserved the comic parts for himself, he must also have played Alceste as a comic character designed to amuse the public. The subtitle *ou l'atrabilaire amoureux* (or The Irritable Lover) indicates that a specifically ridiculous aspect of the character was intended. But a person may only *seem* ridiculous from the blasé point of view of the world or, since we are in the theater, the audience. Ridiculousness arises from incongruity. Alceste's ridiculousness stems from the rigidity and dogmatism of the idealist who declines to adapt himself and thus lets himself in for annoyance, quarrels, and unfriendliness. Such an idealist must ultimately completely break off relationships with all others. In a word, ridiculousness is a consequence of rigid extremism.

Bergson has defined the comic as *"raideur"* (rigidity) and not as *"laideur"* (ugliness). Whether the protagonist is right in principle is less important from the point of view of comedy than the fact that since he is devoid of reasonableness and a sense of reality, he interferes with the functioning of society. Alceste would be a good man if he lived in a world filled with good men like himself. Since other men are irritating and imperfect examples of the species, however, and since society must function with these people and not in opposition to them, he is comic and must run into trouble.

In an introductory scene reminiscent of the expositions of the two *Schools*, Alceste is presented to us in conversation with Philinte, his adaptable, realistically reasoning, worldly opposite. Indeed, in many ways *The Misanthrope* represents a newer variation of these predecessors, although it offers us a nobler, more positive hero and is entirely free of elements of farce. Like Sganarelle and Arnolphe, Alceste is a dissatisfied social critic who would like to change the world instead of changing himself to fit in it. He is a man who will not play along, as the tolerant Philinte advises him to do, because he absolutely cannot bear the game. He has no plan like Sganarelle and Arnolphe, who, because they cannot accept women as they are, want to arrange the education of a particular woman. Alceste has only one tactic: not to play along, but to remain rigorously himself, even if he appears to be ridiculous. And just as Philinte has prophesied, this is exactly what happens.

Alceste's first test comes during his first meeting with Oronte, a bore (*facheux*). The action takes place in the salon of Célimène, Alceste's chosen love; a lady much admired in social circles, she is courted by scores of young gallants. Dramaturgically speaking, we are viewing a point where various lines of society intersect. Oronte is as serious a suitor of Célimène as Alceste, as it turns out. He has composed a sonnet and would like to read it aloud in order to hear Alceste's opinion of it. He is friendly and intent on friendship. For Alceste, this wish for friendship is nothing but a mask. Friendship is no frivolous game of fleeting acquaintanceships. For example, in Alceste's eyes it would be absolutely necessary for true friendship to be able to tolerate honesty or, more specifically, honest criticism. Oronte's vanity in reading the sonnet (which gives Molière the opportunity to make fun of contemporary poetasters) and Alceste's candidly negative judgment (which reflects Molière's conception that lyrical poetry must embody natural simplicity) provide a relatively cheerful interval before the more serious conflicts between the ponderous idealist and Célimène's frivolous acquaintances.

Why, then, does Alceste find himself in a social group with which he evidently has nothing in common—a society in which one is friendly to a person's face but gossips maliciously behind his back, a society in which one merely trifles with feelings and ideas, and in which intrigue is indulged in to one's heart's content? Why does he love a woman who is the opposite both of himself and his ideal image of a human being—a coquette for whom seriousness and honesty are incomprehensible, an artificial being who conducts her life as if it were an aesthetic exercise, a woman in pursuit of pleasure and lacking all sense of responsibility? Does he hope to change society (and his beloved) to fit his own image? Is he looking for trouble? Does he want to put his powers and his concept of life to a test?

Or does he, whom Célimène terms an *ésprit contrariant* (a self-contradicting spirit), simply suffer from a dichotomy between head and heart which obsessively drives him to that very place where he will be most misunderstood, most despised, and most wounded? Does he suffer from a ridiculous masochism which causes him to carry things to a point where he no longer perceives or considers the consequences of his actions and thus destroys himself? He exposes himself in the most unnatural and unreasonable manner. Because he makes no distinction between what is important and what is not, he makes unnecessary enemies of those whom he would like to have as friends. He is the sole "innocent" in a world of "hypocrites."

In the course of the play Molière allows this world to unfold by means of an artfully linked series of tableaux filled with people in various disguises. Alceste, himself, is always present at the edge of the circle, in his dark sulking-corner which becomes ever darker and more isolated until at the very end it has become a "desert." Even the philosophic Philinte and his female counterpart Éliante are "hypocrites," masqueraders, who amicably play along with society's games even though they essentially despise them.

The two vain Marquises—Acaste and Clitandre—are placed as "bores" between Célimène and Alceste. Both are simple marionettes who boastingly indulge in a competitive struggle for favor at court and among women. They angrily leave the scene when Célimène's almost identical letters to them are publicly exposed to have been a malicious joke played at the expense of their vanity.

Another "bore" is Arsinoé, the prude, who, in her effort to drive a wedge between Alceste and Célimène (since she wants him herself and is also jealous of Célimène's youth and success with men), becomes the force that propels the play's dramatic events. She gives Alceste the fatal letter which Célimène has written in tender tones to someone else (to Oronte, as it turns out). Thus the blind lover, who had considered his passion requited, receives incontrovertible proof of the inconstancy of this love and of the fickleness of his beloved. He now openly lays his cards on the table with his "Do you love me? I love you contrary to all reason." This is the very declaration Alceste has been vainly striving to make from the beginning, but was hindered from so doing by constant interruptions from the various bores—as well as by Célimène's skillful tactics of evasion.

Finally, there is Célimène herself. She plays to perfection the charming coquette, the ingeniously witty gossip, and the society lady bent on ingratiating herself with everyone. When necessary, she can also hypocritically and expertly play the role of an honorable lady. Thus, she adapts herself to exposure and admits her faults, but she does not let herself be converted to Alceste's concept of life, nor to that of anyone else. She believes that everything can be easily settled by the mere admission that her intentions were not bad, that she was only indulging in a pleasant diversion.

Alceste, who for his own sake initially urges her to deny what she had done (love temporarily compels even him to suspend his principles), then demands proof of her love; he has been shaken rather than cured by her frivolity. He demands that she belong to him alone, that she join him in forever renouncing amusement and society. Once again he tries to impose upon another something that corresponds to his own ideals but takes no cognizance of reality. How can he for one moment believe that he can transform a co-

quette into a loyal and loving wife, an extrovert into
an introvert, and that he can remove from society a
woman whose sole purpose in life had consisted in
gaining people's admiration and in manipulating them?
However, Célimène parries with the remark: "*La
solitude effraye une âme de vingt ans. . . .*" (Alas, at
twenty one is terrified of solitude.)

The absurdity of Alceste's love having been proven,
he now carries to its ultimate consequence his basic
error of wishing to impose his own will in opposition
to the demands of reality. The result is isolation. Because he is honest, he cannot be satisfied with a substitute love. Nor can he allow another person to feel that
she is herself only a substitute. Thus he also withdraws
apologetically from Éliante, who would willingly have
accepted the hand Alceste had shortly before offered
her because of his anger over Célimène's duplicity.
At the end of the play, Éliante is naturally paired off
with Philinte. Our last glimpse of Célimène shows
her heading for the kind of future which will within a
few years turn her into a woman like Arsinoé. In the
society Molière is describing, a coquette inevitably
becomes a prude as she grows older. Indeed, Célimène herself has analyzed this process with respect to
Arsinoé's behavior.

The play provides yet a second level upon which
Alceste's character is "examined": the ridiculous unreasonableness of his rigid idealism is demonstrated in
the context of that society in which he finds himself
for better or for worse. At the very beginning there is
talk of a lawsuit in which Alceste is involved. More
details are given later when it becomes clear that he is

reputed to be the author of a seditious book. Is he then a writer? Molière's characters, insofar as they are middle or upper-middle class, have no professions. In accordance with the times, they merely shared membership in a particular social class. They circulate in Parisian society or at court, they occupy themselves with the administration of their property or with their literary pretensions. However, the "book" itself may not be the cause of the lawsuit, after all; the nature of the case remains unspecified. We know only that from the very beginning Alceste claims to be in the right, and that Philinte agrees with him. We also know that Alceste's unknown opponent (who is later supported by Oronte after Alceste has disparaged his sonnet) is accused of malicious denunciation and perversion of justice.

Thus even Alceste's opponent at law is a "bore," one of many who are out to annoy Alceste and strengthen his contempt for mankind. But Alceste's conception of justice is an ideal intimately related to his ideal conceptions of social behavior. It is "subjective" and not oriented toward reality. The comedy here is bitter: honor, probity, decency, and the law all oppose his enemy, Alceste rages. The justice of his own case is acknowledged everywhere, and nevertheless the court decides in favor of a man whose scandalous behavior is known by all.

Alceste's attitude here reminds us of his condemnation of the badly-written sonnet: he is concerned with principle and not with success. As long as Alceste knows himself to be in the right, he is not interested in the consequences of his actions. In this fashion he had made an enemy of Oronte. Similarly, he now refrains from further efforts to exact from this earthly administration of justice those things he idealistically feels to be his due. Oronte has Alceste summoned before the court marshals to account for the insult to him. An apology is demanded as would be appropriate in the case of an *honnête homme*. But Alceste is not an *honnête homme* like Philinte who, in keeping with the social code he follows and not in accordance with an absolute concept of honor, sets tolerance and sociability as the measure of all things. Alceste, however, cannot "unsay" those things which he has said out of conviction. The best that he can do is to confess his own difficult nature. And as a concession, he adds the sentence: "Sir, I regret that I'm so hard to please, and I'm profoundly sorry that your lyric failed to provoke me to a panegyric."

The lost lawsuit drives Alceste completely back into his sulking corner. Philinte is all for fighting, for contesting the verdict, and for making further legal appeals. However, with the sour demeanor of the injured idealist, Alceste gives up. He will make no attempt to challenge the verdict. Let it go down to posterity as a proof of the wickedness of his contemporaries. True it will cost him twenty thousand francs, but for that sum he will have the right to rage at human nature and nourish an immortal hatred for it.

In his relationship with Célimène, Alceste behaves exactly as he did when his lawsuit was at issue. He cannot budge one centimeter from the position he has taken; it is totally irrelevant that he is the chief victim of such rigidity. This obstinacy illustrates his mon-

strous egocentricity and dogmatism. And yet, he
designates all of those feelings which go hand in hand
with rigidity as "just." Hatred for mankind, anger at
Célimène's deceit, embitterment against the bores—
all of these emotional reactions are a slap in the face of
reason. Alceste loses himself at the end; since his senses
are no longer ruled by reason, he runs head-on into a
wall.

Under the circumstances the only refuge left such a
man is isolation in the desert, and no one either can or
wants to share it with him. Alceste's desert is meta-
phorical, a state of mind rather than a place; and all of
Molière's great monomaniacs eventually "settle"
there. The only difference between Alceste and the
other ridiculous protagonists is that he has exiled himself voluntarily like an early Christian saint who went
into the desert in search of purity. Arnolphe (*The
School for Wives*) and Harpagon (*The Miser*) end in
the desert against their will.

But in a fundamental sense, these characters (including Alceste) have always resided in such a place.
Psychologically, they all live in the desert of their
own obsessions, obsessions which prevent them from
living in a community in which self-criticism, compromise, and sacrifice are demanded in the general interest. Alceste is "right" since he is able to see through
the joy with which his corrupt society makes compromises. However, being right is of no avail to him.
In the eyes of society, which represents the majority
and everyday reality, he is ridiculous. Purity means
nothing to this society which is more interested in
appearances and masks, *le grimace*. A truthful exis-

tence is only possible in isolation. The play ends in a checkmate. However, Molière adds an ironic silvery ray of hope: Philinte and Éliante declare that they are determined to do everything in their power to save Alceste. From what, we may well ask? From himself or from society?

Amphitryon
(Amphitryon, 1668)

In *The Misanthrope*, Molière had pushed the comedy of manners so far in the direction of satire and doubt that his public—feeling uneasy—rejected the play. The audience rightly surmised that this play had attacked their most fundamental presuppositions. Expecting mildly provocative entertainment and amusement, the spectator felt that he had been served up a bitter joke aimed at himself; for the play's social criticism did not take to task a few ridiculous aspects of human behavior capable of improvement, but attacked the basic structure and substance of society. Despite his comic condemnation of Alceste, it was felt that Molière had placed the weight of his symphathy on the side of his hero, and that he considered Alceste's failure to be the failure of a basically noble man in a corrupt world. This world and its rules of conduct was the world of Molière's audience: the court, bourgeois society, and the precepts and customs of the age. Since the audience was part and parcel of this

world, it was not inclined to damn completely its own
social concepts, as Alceste had done in the comedy.

The Misanthrope was, therefore, a fiasco. However,
Molière learned a lesson for the future from the failure of this play: if he wanted to survive, he could not
indulge his talent in similar attempts at dramatic and
philosophical explorations. His Majesty the Audience,
upon whose favor he depended, would be as little inclined to follow his next effort as it had been to follow
The Misanthrope.

Molière was no idealist like Alceste. During the
scandals surrounding his plays, he did not behave like a
sulky dogmatist; on the contrary, by means of accommodation and skillful string-pulling, he was sooner or
later able to achieve what he set out to achieve. Moreover, he had professionally proclaimed the anti-
Alceste motto: *plaire le public.* Finally, because he did
not wish to sacrifice the favor of the King under
whose generous patronage the troupe had recently
been named *Troupe du Roi* (The King's Players), he
refrained from further travels down a path which had
led him from *Tartuffe* to *Don Juan* and now to Alceste, a path which might yet perhaps lead him into a
dead end from the point of view of comedy. Severely
ill and financially responsible for his family and
troupe, he declared that he would conduct no more
experiments. Much to the pleasure of the King and the
public, he henceforth wrote no more bitter comedies
with quasi-sympathetic heroes.

The motto of his work during the last, most pro-
ductive, and most successful years of his life was: back
to farce (with which he had originally won the pub-

lic's heart) and onwards to ballet-comedy (with which he was to win the acclaim of the court). In a certain sense, society may have triumphed in that it prevented him from probing ever further into the darker recesses of human behavior and developing still more innovative forms of comedy. But he conquered society in turn by giving it more than the conventional comedy it demanded. While doing its bidding, Molière produced poetic and dramatic masterpieces which do not speak for his age alone, but for all times. Molière's compromises may be compared metaphorically to water's victory over stone: he worked on and on, slowly, tenaciously, reasonably, but without giving up his own essential uniqueness.

With his appointment to the post of chief entertainer and organizer of court festivals in Versailles and elsewhere (a post he shared with the Italian Lully), Molière was given an opportunity to create spectacles in the truest sense of the word. For the first time in his career, he was not compelled to keep a watchful eye on box-office receipts. The resulting works demonstrated his various talents for observing human behavior, writing poetically, and creating comic theater; they also fulfilled a challenge to the all-round artist in him to create total artistic creations which simultaneously addressed themselves to the eyes and the ears, to imagination and experience, to mythology and reality. These works, which took full advantage of all of the artistic and theatrical possibilities of the times, offered the public a glittering unity of colors and shapes, sounds and movements, living figures and theatrical machinery. No limits were set, and Molière used this freedom to create brilliant forms of entertainment which integrated comedy, ballet, masquerade, and mechanical spectacle into a coordinated theatrical whole.

The court Molière served was convinced of its participation in a mythical age. This feeling pervaded all of its members from the Sun King himself down to the lowliest servant. Moreover, the chief god in this hierarchy (the King) ordered his subjects to find an artistic expression for it. Parallels were sought in the mythology of past ages and especially the Greco-Roman tradition, which was plundered for symbols and stories that stressed analogies with the present age and legitimized it. In his search for courtly-baroque material for his comedies in the works of Plautus (as well as in those of Rotrou, his own contemporary), Molière found a theme that paid tribute to the King, acknowledged the spirit of this age so possessed with the stage, and made full use of the rich possibilities of the court theater. He rediscovered the tale of Amphitryon and his young wife Alcmene, whom Jupiter had seduced in the guise (and in the absence) of her husband, thereby begetting the demigod Hercules.

As in the case of Don Juan, this story was familiar to the public in every detail (especially since Rotrou's play on the same theme had been staged with great success only a few years before). Therefore, it was a story whose form and artistic details only needed to be given new life by means of verse and the aid of the ingenious theatrical machinery which had recently become fashionable in all plays on mythological subjects. Molière did for the theater what La Fontaine did for Aesops's fables: he transformed the ancient material of the classics into contemporary classical poetry. A glance at Plautus will show the magnificent metamorphosis which took place; an elegant comedy was created from a relatively crude joke.

The free verse in this play is unusual, and while it is still rhymed, it is much more flexible than Alexandrine verse. It gives the entire play a graceful lightness and unusual powers of nuance which compensate for its lack of seriousness. It also serves to characterize precisely the manifold emotions of the dramatic conflict caused by the twofold duplication: Amphitryon-Jupiter and Sosie-Mercury. The comedy is a play of double vision. However, the comic division between appearance and actuality possesses only poetic reality, since the play has been transposed to a purely fantastic plane, away from the real and the moral. For Plautus, Jupiter and Mercury were still figures of religious significance and their capacity to transform themselves into given mortals was an accepted article of faith. In Molière's version of the tale, these figures are purely creatures of imagination.

Molière's portrayal of Jupiter's seduction of the chaste Alcmene does not suggest the remotest applicability of earthly morality. Amphitryon is not a comic figure because he has been cuckolded (a situation which would appear as grotesque in a farce and satirical in a higher form of comedy); he is comical because he becomes the victim of a confusion of identities which the audience is in a position to untangle. Sosie, too, is plunged into this confusion to the delight of the audience. But because this servant and commoner is different in psychological make-up from the princely Amphitryon (i.e., he is timid like Sganarelle in *Don Juan*, a compromiser and hanger-on by profession), Sosie is a much more drastically comic figure who operates on a much lower level than does his master. In order to preserve the dramatic symmetry of the play, Molière has also given Sosie a wife, the prudish Cléanthis. Not knowing to whom she is speaking, Cléanthis accuses Sosie of what is really Mercury's sexual neglect, and she accuses Mercury of the real Sosie's marital tepidness. This provides a delightful secondary plot in the more drastic manner of farce. However, the earthy language of this secondary plot achieves a poetic lightness because Molière has retained the use of free verse even here.

Jupiter has selected the night before Amphitryon's return from battle as his own night of love with Alcmene. Thanks to his omnipotence, the god has also prolonged the duration of this night for his own pleasure. While Jupiter is with Alcmene, the real Sosie, who has preceded from the battlefield, trembles fearfully in the pitch-darkness of this long night, rehearsing both his battle report and Amphitryon's message of love, which he must deliver to Alcmene in the morning.

Mercury, in the guise of Sosie, guards the door to Amphitryon's house, since he has been chosen to keep watch while Jupiter is making love to Alcmene. He now begins a sham fight over the exchange of identities with his double. The result of this duel is that for the sake of peace Sosie is brought to the point of denying his own identity and of neglecting his obligations as a servant. However, he denies his own existence not because of what his eyes have told him, but because Mercury has threatened him with a stick.

Jupiter takes leave of Alcmene and reminds her that he has come to her as a lover and not as a husband. The audience smiles knowingly when it hears this distinction, which is almost insulting to Alcmene who conceives of herself as a faithful wife. However, this distinction is later decisive for Amphitryon. It also contains the play's message, which in the name of his libertine King Molière smilingly passes on to the husbands of those women whom the King loves: the god, the highest lord in the hierarchy, has the right to love whomever he will; he stands outside of human laws and human codes of conduct.

The confusion in this play is subtly maintained over a long period of time by means of an ingenious arrangement of entrances and exits. Indeed, it is not unraveled until the very end of the comedy when Jupiter appears before Amphitryon as a god. (It may be noted here that Jupiter never appears before his human counterpart in his human form, as Mercury does when he appears before Sosie.) This confusion plunges Amphitryon into a series of situations whose contradictory nature tests both his feelings and his reason to near breaking point. Amphitryon is suspicious of Alcmene, and Alcmene distrusts Amphitryon. Both the husband's honor and the wife's chastity seem to have been violated. The constant question "Who are you really" is continually complemented by the question "Who am I really?" (Heinrich von Kleist took such pleasure in Molière's *Amphitryon* that he translated it into German and slightly modified it to suit the more romantic, metaphysical sense of comedy peculiar to his own age. This great nineteenth-century German dramatist was deeply concerned with the mysterious question of human identity, which was the very cornerstone of his poetic meditations.)

Molière does not illuminate the psychological and existential possibilities presented by his theme. Keeping his figures from tragic abyss, he merely allows the implications of this theme to float in the cheerful atmosphere of an allegorical comedy. His Amphitryon, having returned from war and suffered a cool reception from his wife—who supposes him to have just returned to the battlefield—never doubts himself for a moment. He doubts only the honor and prudence of his wife as well as the loyalty and reason of his servant.

Gentle, pious, feminine, and innocent, Molière's Alcmene maintains her integrity in the same manner as her husband maintains his. She angrily rejects Amphitryon's groundless and unjustifiable suspicion; she feels aggrieved when he seems to be cruelly playing with her feelings; she proudly withdraws into herself when his behavior finally seems to her to be incomprehensibly capricious. But these reactions all express the genuine, unadulterated feelings of a loving woman who might have been created by Racine—just as Amphitryon's feelings are those of a nobleman concerned with his honor and his highly respected household.

The cheerful comic aspects of this play arise from the convoluted and complicated situation which a god has created for his own amusement, when he is urged on by caprice and a sudden impulse to trifle. This situation is preserved for three acts; to the delight of the audience—which has been clued in to the real identities of the characters involved—the plot proceeds from crisis to crisis, occasionally even heading toward catastrophe. Jupiter is the father figure. He subordinates the well-being of his children to his desire to beget the demigod Hercules. This was not much different from the lordly way in which the Sun King, Louis XIV, gave his own pleasure precedence over the interests and needs of his subjects. But the play as a whole possesses the magic and elegance of a baroque painting on a mythological subject. It has as little reality as such a painting and therefore lacks that reference to real life which might cause anxiety in its audience.

On the other hand, the play shows as much care as such a painting in its artistic composition, in its contrasting of moods, in its depiction of illusions, and in the presentation of a cheerful kind of verisimilitude. In short, *Amphitryon* resembles a cheerful dream embodied in a cheerful poetic form. It also presents a splendid challenge to both actor and director alike. The play's duplications demand, first of all, each actor's disciplined imitation of the other. And, since the doubles are constantly relieving one another with extreme speed on the stage, the rapid succession of contrasting scenes demand of both the actor and the director utmost sensitivity in their sense of timing.

Georges Dandin
(Georges Dandin, ou Le Mari
confondu, 1668)

Once again Molière had been commis-
sioned to write a play for a court festival; this time it
was to celebrate France's conquest of Franche-Comté
and the Peace of Aachen. Designed to complement a
pastoral verse play which was to be performed out-
doors in a specially constructed *théâtre de verdure*,
Georges Dandin was a revision of his first known play,
a farce entitled *La Jalousie du Barbouillé* (The
Clown's Jealousy), written during Molière's years in
the provinces. The comedy also presented a variation
of the Sganarelle role as it first appeared in *The Imaginary Cuckold*; but the protagonist no longer merely
fancies himself to be a cuckold: In *Georges Dandin*,
he really is one. Therefore, this newer version offers a
bitter variation of the ancient comic theme of marital
conflict, the incompatibility of husband and wife, and
the outwitted husband.

Nevertheless, the play is more than this: it is a comedy of manners in which society as a whole is satirized

as incisively as in *The Misanthrope*; however, since Molière wished to avoid another fiasco, he shrewdly limited his caricature to one sector of society—the provincial aristocracy—and designed his comedy as a farce from which his audience could feel itself far removed. This play contains neither a "sympathetic" hero, nor effusive commentary on the wickedness of man. Moreover, there is no portrayal of a man's attempt to change either the world or his own fate, as the misanthropic Arnolphe and Alceste had attempted to do, the one by means of a cunning plan, the other by remaining inflexibly "himself." In *Georges Dandin*, all of the characters are either ultra-ridiculous or ultra-wicked, from the wretched, deceived husband, Georges Dandin, to his narrow-minded aristocratic in-laws and the two ruthless pairs of lovers—Clitandre and Angélique, Lubin and Claudine (the first pair's go-betweens and confidants).

The plot contains the material for tragedy: Georges Dandin, a rich peasant, has one flaw in his character, snobbism; he therefore marries above his social rank. He must atone for this by becoming a cuckold, by being shut out of his own house and, finally, by being driven to the point of suicide. However, he is a victim who moves us to laughter rather than tears, because in addition to being a snob, he is also stupid. He cannot understand that there is no help for him in his situation, although he knows exactly what is going on behind his back and that neither his coquettish wife nor her seemingly respectable parents can be changed.

The play was a pure delight to court society, which

could make fun of its ridiculous provincial cousins. It was just as amusing to sophisticated Parisian theater-goers who could laugh at the babbling peasant, the boorish provincial snobs, and the risqué triangle presented in the comedy. There was no reason for anyone to feel himself attacked or insulted by the play, but every reason for him to feel splendidly entertained.

Molière had become a master in the construction of his plays. In *Georges Dandin*, he employs a structural principle of farce, the repetition of episodes, but in such a modified manner that the form of the play describes the development of three concentric circles. These circles consist of three similar adventures which taken together provide a gradual progression of events. Dandin's humiliation becomes ever greater and his wife's cunning ever more shameless until the open-ended conclusion of the play is reached: the duped Dandin admits defeat when the net he himself has spun closes around him. Dandin's monologues, which both introduce and conclude each "adventure," frame them and connect them to one another by providing clues to future events and retrospective conclusions; in either case, a deep sigh of self-insight runs through these remarks and provides a leitmotiv which also formulates the comedy's theme: *"Tu l'a voulu!"* (This is what you wanted!)

As in Plautus's comedies, Dandin is at once the protagonist and his own commentator. Comedy and distance are achieved by the manner in which Dandin constantly addresses himself in the third person, points a finger at his actions, and analyzes his own stupidity

and his own misery as if he were talking about someone else. This dramatic device also illustrates the fact
that knowledge is of no help in such situations.

In order to develop the intrigue, Molière makes use
of a trick which is reminiscent of *The School for
Wives*. We may recall here that Arnolphe had been
precisely informed about each phase of any maneuver
that was being carried out against him, and that despite his knowledge he was powerless to intervene.
Dandin, too, stumbles upon the first babbling message
of love being carried between his wife and Clitandre;
he is then informed of each further arrangement and
rendezvous. But although he may eventually be the
wiser for this information, he is no better able to cope
with the present moment. His detailed knowledge
only increases his suffering. He gradually becomes
ever more conscious of his impotence until, having
been brought down a peg, he comprehends that his
will has been crippled by circumstances.

It is as though we are observing the dancing movements of a fly's struggle to free itself from a spider's
web, as the spider looks on with amusement. Dandin
makes several attempts to save himself. He appeals to
his in-laws, letting them know that he has sound evidence against his wife and promising to give it to them
so that they can call their adulterous daughter to account. However, his efforts always fail because his
simple peasant cunning is not equal to the intrigues of
the daughter from a higher social class. Moreover, this
provincial aristocracy, basing its judgments solely
upon appearances, is more inclined to believe one of
its own members than someone of a different class—

even though the former is telling the most obvious lies.

Georges Dandin's snobbism is "the world's greatest folly," as he himself admits. Because of it he chose a wife with his eyes shut and was unaware that she had claws. Blinded by superficial brilliance, Dandin has allowed himself to purchase a pig in a poke; he does not know whether he has received good value or bad until he tries to use it.

The blindness with which Dandin believes in the decency of his in-laws until the very last moment is almost touching. It naturally makes him unable to see through their empty babbling about family trees, honor, codes of conduct, etc. As the incurable victim of his own class prejudices, he accepts their stupid manner of argumentation and their aristocratic concept of how people are to be addressed and how apologies are to be made. (Of course, such mannerisms of speech in the mouth of a crude peasant are a grotesque incongruity.) The very people whom he believes to be his greatest allies are in reality his greatest humiliators. They take his identity away from him and force him to behave as they do, although they continue to treat him as an inferior member of a lower order. Since the snob usually attaches himself to false models, Dandin's in-laws are not exactly shining examples of the superiority of their class. Indeed, there is in reality very little superiority to be seen in the manner in which these people have unquestioningly sold their daughter for money, or in the way in which they believe in absolute adherence to the letter of form.

Georges Dandin's bad luck with his wife is not to be

explained solely on the basis of his snobbism. It must also be viewed in the light of the bourgeois concept of marriage which allows a man to enter the state of matrimony without taking into consideration the will and inclination of his partner. Angélique, who is not an Agnès but rather a provincial Célimène, has something to say on this subject (Act II, Scene 2). Once again Molière champions the cause of proper education for girls, though he does so less innocently in *Georges Dandin* than in both *Schools*; for in *Georges Dandin*, a wife actually betrays her husband, while in the *Schools* the young girls finally select their natural partners by themselves. Angélique gets off scot-free with her infidelity. Molière motivates her actions by explaining them as being the natural need of a frustrated young girl for a genuine sentimental adventure. Like the ridiculous snobs Magdelon and Cathos (in *The Precious Damsels*), Angélique rebels against the bourgeois and materialistic manner of treating daughters and wives as merchandise, a custom also in vogue among impoverished aristocrats. Dandin speaks like Gorgibus in *The Precious Damsels*, like Sganarelle in *The School for Husbands*, and like Arnolphe in *The School for Wives*, when he says in effect: "I am your husband and I am letting you know that I have a different view of things." And Angélique responds like all young girls in a Molière comedy: "And I am your wife and am letting you know that I will stand by my point of view."

In this manner, two opposing wills clash head-on, and the stronger and shrewder will is victorious. Angélique does not possess the sweetness and depth of feeling inherent in some of Molière's other young girls; she is an egotistical coquette who is more interested in playing with feelings than in the feelings themselves. Her lover Clitandre is an empty-headed creature who dances to her tune. She spins all of the threads of the intrigue almost entirely on her own. Her sole confederate is the maid Claudine, her equally sly but cruder counterpart. Claudine is in turn aided by her own lover Lubin (Clitandre's servant), a fool whom she delights in wrapping around her little finger.

All in all, Molière gives us a rather terrifying picture of humanity in this play. Each character is unscrupulously out for himself at the cost of everyone else. The representatives of that society which stands in opposition to the comic hero are hard creatures devoid of sympathy. The moderating voice of reason in the person of a *raisonneur* is missing from this work, and the intriguers, whose goal is both immoral and destructive of social order, get away scot-free with their actions. (In this, they represent a contrast to the intriguers in other Molière comedies, who pursue their goals in the interest of order.)

It is important to note that Molière spares his public moral indignation by allowing this comedy's intrigue to develop in the manner of an enormous joke. It is an ingenious game of hide-and-seek played in quick time, in which the faster and more cunning player always has the lead. Georges Dandin is forever running behind his intended victim, and each time that he thinks he is about to catch his prey, it eludes him. The individual episodes of this game are traditional.

First, there is the underhanded way in which the lovers exchange coded messages of love under the very eyes of both Dandin and his puritanical in-laws. Second, there is the way in which they transform each trap set for them into a noose for Dandin. Third, there is the manner in which Dandin always arrives somewhere just a bit too late. Finally, there is the manner in which entrances and exits are timed in such a way that Angélique can cover her retreats by means of improvisation. All these episodes belong to the situation comedy of farce.

The grotesque confusion is heightened as the play develops towards its last scene. Since this scene takes place at night, Molière employs that old trick of allowing his characters to run into the very people they least expect to meet. For example, Lubin thinks that Dandin is Claudine and kisses his hand. However, this device illustrates drastically and graphically the lack of communication (both verbal and physical) depicted in the play as a whole. The lively game of cat-and-mouse alternates between the house and the street. Angélique's superb game of masks is crowned at the moment when she is caught by her angry husband in the midst of a nocturnal rendezvous with Clitandre and is locked out of the house. With a glib tongue, she most convincingly appeals to Dandin's sympathy but is not quite successful. Realizing that this appeal will not help her, she promptly feigns death. This desperate measure has the desired effect and reverses the situation immediately. Angélique is now safely inside the house and Dandin, the defeated dupe, is locked out.

The play's tempo conceals its cruel and melancholy

content. When Georges Dandin is compelled for the second time to repeat an apologetic litany to his father-in-law, Monsieur de Sotenville, and to beg forgiveness from his wife, who simply cannot be outwitted, he throws in the sponge. He gives up all hope, because he knows that there is no further help for him. By this time, however, the complicated action and the laughter it provokes has reduced the audience to a state of breathlessness. With no more than a blink of the eye, it takes note of Dandin's despairing exit thought—"if one has married a bad woman, as I have, one cannot do anything more reasonable than to plunge into water head-first and drown oneself." It is no longer really touched by the thrice-repeated "Oh" of this petty peasant who has been locked out of his house, brought to his knees, and humbled in the eyes of the world.

This is the spirit of farce in which great delight is taken in tormenting someone for his stupidity, ugliness, ineptitude, or inarticulateness. The victim is harassed, humiliated, laughed at, isolated, and driven to such depths of despair that suicide seems the sole comfort left him. Molière gave his blockhead more personality than was customarily seen in the traditional comic peasant. Indeed, his basic humanity makes him come alive for us. But Molière alienated the spectator's sympathy for Dandin by making betrayal, injustice, adultery, and even suicide, appear ridiculous.

The Miser
(L'Avare, 1668)

The figure of the bourgeois lies at the center of Molière's comedies. (This is not surprising, since the bourgeois really plays a central role in all comedies.) Though his typical characteristics and ideals—individualism, sense of family, industriousness, energy, and realism—can be strengths, if they are dogmatically carried to excess they become weaknesses revealing a common denominator of self-centeredness and egotism. The bourgeois represents the essence of a type who insists on the primacy of an ego that blindly strives to control its environment and treats everything as mere chattel. His excesses result from overweening complaisancy and a corresponding lack of flexibility. His rigidity causes him to idolize his ego and to nurture it so relentlessly in every way (materially, financially, gastronomically, and sexually) that his humanity is lost in the process. Moreover, his rigidity leads to the destruction of social equilibrium, that is to say, the balance among existent interpersonal relationships, and paralyzes the natural development of other people's lives and interests.

From Aristophanes to Brecht, the portrayal of such weaknesses was a fundamental element of comedy. Dramatically intensified and artistically stylized, the portraits all retained an essential core of realism. And yet, as classical aesthetics optimistically emphasized, such illustrations of human weaknesses were not primarily intended to mend mores but to entertain both the educated classes and the common man. As the middle class began its social climb, these plays were also meant to entertain the bourgeoisie itself.

In Molière's time the bourgeoisie, a solid wedge between the common people (the peasants and servants) and the already shaky aristocracy, faced the future full of confidence. It already possessed all of the faults and vices of the wealthy and powerful, of those who "had arrived." The *bonhomme*, having reached middle or advanced age, autocratically transformed his ideals into dogmas, which he then rigidly and tyrannically applied to serve his own interest, disregarding not only the welfare of the majority but, indeed, the welfare of his own family. As a strict *pater familias*, as a moralizer, and as a wheeler-dealer, he confidently sought to exploit others; but as Molière's comedies demonstrate, in the final analysis his behavior was self-damaging. Lacking consideration for others, he himself becomes less fully human and suffers a loss in his personal relationships and in the intensity of his spiritual and emotional life. His wish to control his dependents provokes a corresponding desire for freedom on the part of the suppressed. If freedom is not

voluntarily conceded to them, they procure it for
themselves in underhanded ways. Therefore, the stubborn bourgeois meets with rebellion on all sides. Rebellious wives, children, and servants fight with every
means in their power for their right to live as they
choose and to protect their vital interests.

There is no critical agreement as to why the conflicts thus provoked within the bourgeois's small domestic world are comical. It is easier to experience
than to explain the pleasure derived from the fall of an
unsuspecting victim. Why the exposure of weaknesses
and presumptuous attitudes causes laughter can only
be explained in terms of another human weakness:
gloating over other people's misfortunes. Just as a kind
of masochism is involved in weeping, so, too, is a form
of sadism implied in laughter. We feel quite far removed from the figure we are laughing at, and the
comical *bonhomme* is a person quite different from
ourselves. We would not like to be such a person; at
the same time, we try by disowning him to destroy in
ourselves those traits that we share with him. Thus his
suffering becomes the source of our pleasure.

Based on a model by Plautus, *The Miser* is a comedy
of middle-class life par excellence. The unbearable
tensions of a middle-class family, which is arbitrarily
and selfishly dominated by a father, turn into a bitter
game of ruthless command and clandestine disobedi-
ence. The whole play would end in a checkmate, if
Molière had not devised an imaginatively romantic
conclusion that artificially restores order and equilibrium.

The family life of the miserly Harpagon and his

totally intimidated children, Cléante and Élise, reflects a vicious world in which no one trusts anyone. In opposing the imperious and powerful Harpagon, who obsessively keeps watch over his money, all of the other characters in the play become swindlers and hypocrites. They try to cheat him out of things which he rightly owes them but withholds out of monstrous greed and self-love. The bourgeois household becomes a cave and the bourgeois father a monster. His oppressed dependents who share the cave are thus forced, on the one hand, to employ the most subtle forms of cunning against him and, on the other hand, to constantly fall in with his whims and moods in order to scrape together the barest form of existence. They play the roles in which he has cast them, but behind his back they strive for a little independence, a little pleasure, and a few centimeters of maneuvering space. The childrens' destroyed relationship to their father destroys all other human relationships. Their love affairs are clandestinely nurtured: Élise's affair with Valère takes place in her own home but under false pretences, since Valère simultaneously plays the role of Harpagon's major domo.

As the play opens, we learn that Valère has probably been permitted to "seduce" Élise in order to obtain a secure pledge of her love. This is an enormous novelty in Molière's work. Sexuality is generally treated with strict propriety and mostly by way of allusion; it is rarely the object of a joke and still more seldom the material for a play's conflict. Although jealousy, love, and coquettry play a central role, these phenomena are presented more from a psychological than from a physical point of view. Such a treatment of sexuality accords with the prevailing taste of Molière's age: preciosity and courtliness control and conceal man's physical nature. In *The Precious Damsels*, Magdelon's horror of marriage, which demands that a woman sleep with a totally naked man, is a grotesque exaggeration which, however, contains more than a kernel of truth. For even the smallest of ambiguities— such as when Agnès in *The School for Wives* says: *Il m'a pris le . . .* (He has taken my . . .)—shocked the prudes and the oversensitive.

Harpagon's children have the desire, but not the power, to bring their love to fruition in marriage. The father, like every bourgeois of his time, has the sole and final say in this matter. His assent is not directed to fulfilling the wishes of his children; rather, it is dictated entirely according to his own self-interest and avarice. Élise is to marry the rich Anselme, a man Harpagon's age, who has been accorded her hand because he is willing to take her, "sans dot" (without a dowry). For Molière's bourgeois (from Gorgibus in *The Precious Damsels* to Argan in *The Imaginary Invalid*), children are nothing more than an appendage to oneself or a function of one's own interests; they are merchandise that one exchanges for equally valuable (or, if possible, more valuable) goods.

The conflict between generations has rarely been portrayed with such unrelenting bitterness as in *The Miser*. Molière observes his characters with psychological precision: in a house devoid of love, the humbled children become either dreamers or despondent. For example, Cléante reverses his father's miserliness and becomes a spendthrift, while the old-maidish Élise becomes fainthearted. All friends, servants, and visitors are forced into malicious duplicity. Everything is out of joint. Harpagon has power because he has money; his authority stems from the strongbox which he has buried in the garden. This strongbox gives him the courage and confidence with which to tyrannize his children, to court Cléante's girl friend Mariane, and to scold his servants. When the strongbox disappears, his authority goes with it.

Harpagon is a possessed bourgeois who has become a monster. Aggression, irritability, distrust, cunning, and exultant tyranny alternate in him, the one monotonous constant being his fear of being robbed. He always has one ear pitched toward the garden while he is dealing with the various people in his environment. This explains his short, brusque, often disconnected and distracted speech. He only half listens to what people are saying to him. He is impatient and never understands anything fully. He trusts only two people, and ironically enough both are swindlers.

This is, of course, characteristic of those who are permanently distrustful, for gullibility is the other side of suspicion. The suspicious person is always taken in by those who tell him the crassest lies and act as if they were on his side. Valère pretends that he is running Harpagon's household as frugally as his master wishes, but he has already taken Harpagon's most valuable possession, namely, his daughter. Frosine, the matchmaker who takes charge of Harpagon's negotiations with Mariane, impresses us with her cunning as she plays upon the miser as if on an instrument. She manages to encourage his weaknesses, vanity and avarice, without ever arousing his suspicion. And these two alone, Valère and Frosine, win Harpagon's trust.

Isolated by his obsession, in the final analysis Harpagon is a solitary man. He lives without human contact in his topsy-turvy world of distorted values, in his self-made prison, as it were. His lack of "good sense" is as monstrous as Malvolio's in *As You Like It*, and he can just as easily be hoodwinked into believing that his foolish getup represents the latest fashion or that his girl friend would prefer to see him in spectacles. The absurd calculation which Frosine artfully devises in order to persuade Harpagon that the penniless girl whom he has chosen (Mariane) will actually bring in twelve thousand a year because her thrifty ways will save him that sum, accords with Harpagon's credulity as well as with his narrow literal-mindedness. So, too, does Valère's suggestion that they should economize on the wedding feast, because after all, "One must eat to live and not live to eat." (In his enthusiasm, Harpagon puts the cart before the horse and repeats mechanically: "One must live to eat.")

Harpagon is not stupid (otherwise he would merely be the bourgeois of farce such as Euclio in Plautus's *Pot of Gold*, Molière's model). Rather, Harpagon is pigheaded and this quality gives him the vitality and verisimilitude necessary in a figure of comedy. He has an obtuse, egocentric view of the world and thus he fails to judge men and events correctly. His sole test of a person is: "Is he after my money?" or "Can I get money out of him?" He never asks: "What do I owe him?" or, perish the thought, "What does he need?"

He is not a snob and speaks the same language to both his servants and his peers, always anxiously intent on one thing only—how to gain advantage for himself at the expense of others. This eternally distrustful soul is constantly trying to discover whether anyone knows that he has money, that he has hidden it, and where. This gives rise to dialogues that are patterned like dances: the partners in conversation speak past each other, engage each other briefly, separate once again, reach a dramatic climax, and then exit from the stage. Harpagon is always certain of victory; his opponents (Cléante, Frosine, the cook-coachman Jacques) are always frustrated by his obduracy.

As long as Harpagon feels umbilically attached to his beloved strongbox, he appears unassailable, hard, and as immovable as a mountain. The strongbox is his life, his child, his beloved. His relationship to this money is conducted with utmost intimacy and privacy in a world from which even his children are excluded. Thus it is not surprising that the horrific confrontation between father and son at the broker's house (Act II, Scene 2) leaves no lasting impression on Harpagon. And this is despite the fact that Cléante has seen his father as a moneylender of the worst sort and Harpagon has seen his son as a reckless borrower who squanders in the expectation of his father's early death.

Because Harpagon does not love his son, he is not ashamed when Cléante unmasks him: "What, father? Is it you who lend yourself to these shameful actions? . . . Is it you who are trying to enrich yourself by such criminal usury?" Instead he is furious to learn that Cléante is involved in secret financial dealings:

"What, you scoundrel? Is it you who abandon your-self to these criminal adventures? Is it you who are trying to ruin yourself by such disgraceful borrow-ings?" When these two next meet (as Mariane is being introduced into Harpagon's house) the old father-son relationship is restored; it is as bad as ever but no worse. Harpagon and Cléante play the same game of cat and mouse in which the former's bad-tempered insults are met with the latter's cautious and calculated appeasement until the scene reaches its climax. How-ever, in this scene the dramatic highpoint is caused by an outside factor. The assembled company decides that it would like to go out for a drive, but Har-pagon's horses have no horseshoes.

The generational conflict running through the en-tire play remains intangible until the fourth act, when it centers upon Mariane and finally explodes in a viru-lent, malicious manner. Cléante falls into the trap his father has slyly set him. Harpagon cleverly sounds out his son about marriage, and Cléante really believes for a moment that the old man has come to his senses and is about to give him Mariane. Thus he confesses a love which he had heretofore expressed only in comically ambiguous terms—although both the audience and all the other characters but Harpagon know that he loves Mariane. (Cléante: "Allow me, Madame, to put my-self in my father's place and admit to you that . . . the happiness of possessing you is in my eyes the fairest of all fortunes; I set my whole ambition on that." Harpagon: "Gently, son, if you please." Cléante: "It's a compliment I'm paying for you to Madame.")

When Harpagon now hears Cléante's genuine confession of love, he foams with rage, refers to the obedience due a father, and threatens his son with a stick. At this point Jacques, the eternally clumsy go-between, tries to play his role once again but fails as usual. Only the spectator sees unfolding before him an amusing scene filled with profound misunderstandings; it is the lull before the storm. Like Orgon in *Tartuffe*, the bourgeois who has met with resistance considers the most extreme form of revenge: he banishes and curses his son. Goethe has called this scene "fundamentally tragic . . . because the vicious relationship between father and son cancels devotion and respect."

But neither Cléante nor Harpagon are tragic figures. The drastic annulment of their relationship is executed in a tone of choreographical lightness: Harpagon: "I abandon you." Cléante: "Abandon all you like." Harpagon: "I disown you as my son." Cléante: "So be it." Harpagon: "I disinherit you." Cléante: "Whatever you like." Harpagon: "And I give you my curse." Cléante: "Keep it; I don't want anything coming from you."

Since Harpagon's inability to love is well-known to everyone from the very beginning, and thus legitimizes Cléante's rebellion, this scene does not strike the spectator as some terrible event, but rather as the ultimate consequence of a grotesque development. Both of the participants in the conflict are exaggerated and their feelings overdone. The cancellation of devotion and respect may cause us a shudder; however, it neither shocks nor deeply affects us.

The same can be said of the famous monologue in

which the old man discovers that the strongbox has been stolen and expresses his suffering directly to the audience (Act IV, Scene 7), crying *"Au voleur, au voleur!"* (Stop thief!). "Thieves! Robbers! Assassins! Murderers!" Molière carries his comedy at this point to the very edge of pity and fear, but Harpagon's madness is very different from King Lear's, for example. When Lear loses his most beloved possession, his despair stirs profound doubts in him, leads him to introspection and humility, and makes him understand the world's suffering in terms of his own. Harpagon's loss, on the other hand, makes him blinder and even more egocentric. He becomes more comically grotesque than ever. The rhythm of his gasping utterances conveys his grief and his horror; his speech is breathless and staccato; words come out of his mouth in a disconnected manner; he runs about aimlessly; he converses with imaginary people; and he is so beside himself that he feels his own arm as if it were some foreign object.

These reactions reach their climax in Harpagon's monumentally desperate turning on the audience, on the world, as it were, with the full force of his hate and suspicion on all mankind. The content of his passionate monologue corresponds to his horribly confused state of mind. Every sentence, every conclusion is driven to its extreme so that all meaning is inverted to nonsense and absurdity: "Oh dear, my dear, darling money, my beloved, they've taken you away from me and now you are gone I have lost my strength, my joy, and my consolation. It's all over with me. There's nothing left for me to do in the world. I can't go on living without you. It's the finish. I can't bear any more. I'm dying; I'm dead—and buried. (. . . .) I'll call in the law. I'll have everyone in the house put to torture; menservants, maidservants, son, daughter, everyone—myself included. (. . . .) Come on! Come quickly! Magistrates, police, provosts, judges, racks, gibbets, hangmen. I'll have everybody hanged, and if I don't get my money back, I'll hang myself too."

But there is truth comically packaged in this absurdity: people have indeed cut Harpagon's throat in tak-piles words together, intensifying his feelings in every ing his money from him. His identity is so intimately bound up with the strongbox, with his money, with his "beloved," that he falls apart when it is taken from him. His *raison d'être* gone, his very reason goes with it. He therefore loses control of his thoughts and his speech. The latter becomes purely emotional, mere automatic responses. But no one word is strong enough to express his suffering. Therefore, he merely sentence until he ultimately arrives at the notion of self-destruction. The loss of his money has robbed him of the last remnant of his sense of reality; it has also precluded any possibility of being able to relate to others. Only the most extreme reactions are left him: destruction and extinction.

Thus he has lost both himself and his world. His indescribable horror reduces him to a state of inarticulateness. From now on, and throughout the entire fifth act, he is increasingly obsessed, but he continues his incomprehensible attempts to speak. He lives in a desert, far, far away from all other people, and he will continue to do so until he retrieves his lost money. He can neither perceive nor think of anything else; any-thing not connected with the theft passes by him un-noticed. He refers everything said to him to his strongbox and its loss; he swallows Jacques's crude lies, and he misunderstands Valère's confession. In a long scene between Valère and Harpagon, in which both grotesquely speak past each other, the truth about the stolen money is gradually brought to light. Here once again Harpagon carries everything to ex-cess, because only the most severe concepts of punish-ment correspond to his extremely aroused feelings. Thus he gets hopelessly muddled as he utters his ridic-ulous threats: "I was wrong when I said the gallows. You shall be broken on the wheel." And, of course, he calls this "justice."

His ability to make distinctions vanishes; he cannot differentiate between his daughter and his money; everything signifies "murder." He only begins to come to himself when Anselme, Molière's fantastic *deus ex machina*, appears. Anselme not only resolves the seemingly insoluble confusion, but he also meets Harpagon's demands for money with willing accep-tance to pay. Harpagon ignores the wonderful revela-tion of identities which takes place at the end. (It may be recalled that the identities revealed at the end are intimated in the very first scene between Valère and Élise. For this reason it is indefensible to cut this scene in favor of a direct introduction of Harpagon, as often happens in modern productions of *The Miser*. To con-sider this scene merely as old-fashioned exposition is to misunderstand Molière's dramaturgical technique which carefully builds up a composition from causally connected links.) His illogical participation in the conversation remains fixed to the words "money, strongbox, money." He has forgotten Mariane; he cannot assent to Cléante's suggestion to choose between Mariane and the money; there is no choice involved for him. He can think only of money, money, money. Who will pay for the wedding? Who will pay for his wedding suit? Who will pay the notary's fees? He only wants to get back his dear strongbox. The play ends in peace only when Harpagon retakes possession of his strongbox, that is to say, when he has retrieved his life, his reason for existence, his beloved —and his monstrous obsession.

Monsieur de Pourceaugnac
(Monsieur de Pourceaugnac, 1669)

Molière's contemporaries called him "chief farce-player of France." In giving him this title, they merely expressed what the theatrical history of his works demonstrates: Molière's success and fame in his own day derived from his masterful control and extension of the popular genre of farce. Before Molière, farces were mostly a matter of improvisation; hardly ever written down, they enjoyed an ephemeral life at annual country fairs, on the stages of traveling theaters, and in Paris around the Pont Neuf. Molière gave this genre style and form; he made it into a high art which delighted the ultra-refined tastes of court society as well as the most respectable burghers.

Molière combined the vital tempo of the Italian farce (represented by the *commedia dell'arte*) with the realism and wealth of differing types found in the French popular tradition. He refined the dialogue, systematized the gestures, sought to establish a dramatic structure, and created a prototype which later dramatists were able to adapt to their own ages without having to create very much that was new. Evidently, Molière's apprenticeship in the provinces had taught him many tricks and dramatic methods; it also provided him with many basic situations and plots. When it was necessary for him to fulfill a commission quickly or fill a gap in his troupe's repertoire, he drew on this experience and created a farcical plot which wove together various familiar scenes and episodes. From the basic material of this popular tradition, Molière instinctively created something new which bore his own unmistakable signature. Although we know that his great and elegant comedies were slowly and carefully written (writing was, in fact, difficult for him), the farces were created with extreme speed— less on paper than on the very boards of the stage where they were to be performed.

The King was well aware of this talent possessed by his *Valet de Chambre* and chief entertainer. When there was something to celebrate at court, he quickly ordered something with which he could entertain his guests. *Georges Dandin* was such a piece of commissioned entertainment; now came *Monsieur de Pourceaugnac*, a farce derived from a similar basic idea but mounted with cheerful lightness as an amusing ballet-comedy. In other words, the bitter and serious intention underlying *Georges Dandin* was left out of this farce. In *Monsieur de Pourceaugnac*, Molière used a time-honored device to create his comedy: he assembled characters who spoke different "languages" (e.g., dialects, professional jargons, affected turns of phrase) and arranged them around a central comic figure (who also spoke a comical language). The play also contained an intrigue with its dupe, a clandestine love affair involving two suitors and a strict father, various ingenious accomplices, and a colorful crowd of masked dancers. *Monsieur de Pourceaugnac* is meant to be pure entertainment, and it is unconcerned with moral or philosophical problems.

A man from the provinces arrives in Paris. He has set out to court and win as a wife, Julie, the daughter of a rich Parisian bourgeois. The girl, however, has already fallen in love with Eraste, a handsome young man of whom, unfortunately, her father does not approve, and who can only achieve his goal if he can eliminate the provincial suitor. Sbrigani, a resourceful Neapolitan (Scapin's predecessor) promises the young man to work out a foolproof plan whereby Monsieur de Pourceaugnac will be sent packing, and putting their heads together they set to work. Eraste intercepts Monsieur de Pourceaugnac and under false pretenses lures him into his house as his guest. Here, he gives the unfortunate provincial over to two quack doctors and an apothecary who delights in giving enemas. After subjecting Pourceaugnac to all sorts of medical hocus-pocus, they represent him to his future father-in-law as an invalid incapable of marriage and reproduction.

Sbrigani has, in the meanwhile, introduced himself to the father-in-law as Monsieur de Pourceaugnac's creditor who has come to demand payment. He then engages three women who, speaking appropriate dialects, accuse Pourceaugnac of being a bigamist, a philanderer who abandons his victims. Pourceaugnac, oppressed on all sides and surrounded by lies, attempts to procure justice. However, the advocates Sbrigani has hired only lead him by the nose once again. Attempting to escape from Paris disguised as a woman, Pourceaugnac is recognized. Sbrigani buys his freedom —with Pourceaugnac's own money—and sends him on his way. By now, Pourceaugnac is only too happy to be free of this witches' cauldron and is very grateful to Sbrigani for his help. With dramatic irony, he tells Sbrigani: "You are the only honorable man whom I have met in this city."

Oronte, the father of the love-sick Julie, now falls into Sbrigani's net, because he has been made to believe that his daughter has run after her grotesque suitor. Sbrigani pretends to fetch her back. Oronte now wishes to marry her off as soon as possible, since her virtue has become questionable. The situation plays directly into Eraste's hands. All's well that ends well.

An artistically interwoven arrangement of comic situations and comic language adorns the complicated basic plot of this farce, in the course of which nearly all of the traditional figures of the *commedia dell'arte* appear: the father, the young lovers, the grotesque suitor, the servant, the doctor, the soldier, the lawyer. This dramatic ornamentation derives largely from the play's double vision, that is to say, from the division between appearance and reality, mask and true face. It consists largely of ironies which have been given a sharp profile by gross exaggeration. Pourceaugnac is a ridiculously exaggerated *parvenu*. A colorfully dressed and conceited aristocrat, he pompously spews out all sorts of expressions mindlessly garnered from books. He is, above all, easy to outwit. Falling into every trap Eraste and Sbrigani devise, he is the helpless victim of the entire procession of grotesque and unreal figures who obstruct his way, one after another. In successive and interconnected scenes, the ridiculousness of his type as well as the ridiculousness of the doctor, the apothecary, the soldier, and the policeman is systematically exposed. Molière deals doctors a particularly vigorous blow with his portrait of the two swaggering, self-righteous quacks and the apothecary. Eager to apply their favorite but absurd remedies, they know nothing about diagnosis and are basically uninterested in finding a cure. Delivered up to these quacks by Sbrigani and Eraste, Pourceaugnac is as valuable to them as a guinea pig as a truly sick man would be.

The farce thrives on such inversions of truth. Even justice is exaggeratedly presented in a reversal of its function. Farce also thrives on disguise and masquerade, on equivocal language, and on the tempo with which it races from ·one situation to another. Molière separates the various situations by means of grotesque ballet interludes. As the resistant Pourceaugnac is being threatened with an enema, the masked doctors dance around him, reinforced by clowns armed with giant syringes. Later, the lawyers and their assistants sing and dance to the tune of their damnation of polygamy.

In speech, gesture, and pantomime, the whole farce is a matter of caricature. The play distorts, intensifies, and accelerates the normal pace of life; Sbrigani directs and varies the course of the whole enormous joke. Pourceaugnac gradually loses both his reason and his sense of identity. He is confronted with a kind of monstrous counterpart of himself which he cannot get rid of. A final lyrical refrain which, like the lyrical prelude to the play, sings the praises of love in rococo style, brings the bizarre but jolly tumult to a cheerful conclusion. Unnaturalness has been defeated by something natural and everyone awakens from the confusion of a grotesque nightmare.

The Would-Be Gentleman
(Le Bourgeois gentilhomme, 1670)

For centuries critics believed that Molière's greatness was due to the way in which he created characters of convincing verisimilitude. We now take a somewhat different view, since we no longer believe that the theater should be an imitation of life. Therefore, we analyze the structural principles of the drama itself and discover three important things about Molière: an unusual insight into the practical possibilities of the theater; an enormous talent for structural composition; and finally, a subtle sense of how reality can be transformed into theatrical plausibility, something "artificial" which gives the appearance of being natural. The great comedies in particular exemplified Molière's "realism" for critics of past centuries, but these works have as little naturalism in them as do the ballets and farces; in them reality has merely undergone a less obvious artistic metamorphosis, so that at first sight they appear to possess a greater verisimilitude.

164

Modern criticism tends to comprehend Molière's dramaturgy and acting style in terms of the ballet-comedy, that form which dominated the second half of his creative activity. His royal patron, his contemporaries, and generations of theatergoers all agree that it was in this area that Molière accomplished his best and most individual work. Critic Ramon Fernandez's observation that "every scene in a Molière play is at once an illustration and a dance," refers not only to those works in which there is actually dancing on the stage, but rather to a basic principle of Molière's dramaturgy: crystallization of a situation through pantomime, stylized simplification of reality, primacy of theatrical elements.

Of course, the ballet-comedies were commissioned works and thus the products of necessity, as it were. They were often the result of Molière's collaboration with Gian Battista Lully, the Italian composer, and frequently written on themes provided by the King himself. However, these works were no less an expression of Molière's artistic personality and artistic intentions than were the great comedies stemming from his own spontaneous creative impulse. Indeed, one is tempted to add here that the great comedies represent only one aspect of his talent, albeit the more profound one, whereas the ballet-comedies realize the varied nature of Molière's talent: fantasy and humor, realism and playfulness, theatricality and contemplativeness.

No play illustrates this point better than *The Would-Be Gentleman*. Here, a full-blooded comedy about a social snob arose from the King's desire to see Turkish ceremonies presented on the stage in the form of a ballet. (*Turquoiserie* was fashionable at the time as a result of the visit of a Turkish potentate to Louis XIV's court and after the extravagant travel reports by Chevalier d'Arvieux, who also functioned as a Turkish translator at court.) However, Molière produced something quite French from an idea which began as something exotic and foreign. The spectacular Turkish ceremony at the end of *The Would-Be Gentleman* provides its colorful climax, but not the essence of the comedy. Molière skillfully placed the King's theme at the periphery of the play and anchored it as a colorful conclusion to one of his time-honored themes: the theme of the conceited bourgeois. Georges Dandin is resurrected in Monsieur Jourdain, but on a more fantastic plane, in more extravagant costumes, and with more ridiculous pretensions. Dark and bitter tones are totally missing from this later work. In an extensive and cheerful panorama, the play reveals many aspects of the theme of the *parvenu*, using the steps of a ballet augmented by the sensual delights of a costume piece. The comedy makes small claim to plausibility, there is a minimum of story and intrigue, and each narrative element, "having been seen before," is already very familiar. It is theater in a completely un-Aristotelian sense, since its effectiveness is the result of a combination of various artistic elements rather than the result of a dominant plot, theme, or character.

Jourdain is a rich bourgeois who wants to become a nobleman by hook or by crook. He is not really a character, but rather an idea whose actions on the stage suggest those of a comic puppet. He is as much a mask as Mascarille (indeed, many of the scenes and puns have been taken from *The Precious Damsels*). Like Mascarille, he exhibits the same ignorant affectations of culture, the same vanity in dress and artistic achievements. To use a term from photography, Jourdain is shown in continual close-up, and therefore dominates the play. He is a mask whose characteristics have been distorted into the grimaces of a larger-than-life egotist, a madman, if you like, but an amusing one. Although he, too, has his vices, he is merely ridiculous and not in the least dangerous.

Bourgeois materialism, which Harpagon's avarice illustrated in its most extreme form, is also the basis of Jourdain's egotism. However, Jourdain seeks to conceal and to conquer his materialistic nature by adopting an attitude of aristocratic intellectuality. But like all Molière's snobs he mistakenly conceives of the gentleman's mentality as something that can be bought and worn like a coat; that is to say, he considers it not as something innate and essential, but as something accidental. He strains for appearances. Comedy thus arises from the profound incongruity between Jourdain's superficial—purchased—aristocratic airs and his persistently bourgeois nature. All the other characters in the play consider him to be a bourgeois; he alone views himself as a nobleman. This isolates him. Thus although he is an amusing monomaniac, he, too, is a loner in his world of private fantasies.

This is underscored in a series of tableaux which in a cumulative way carry the proverb "clothes make the man" *ad absurdum*. The apotheosis of this motto is the Turkish masquerade in which the bourgeois is fan-

tastically "ennobled"; his pretensions immediately col-
lapse like burst balloons. The clear voices of the genuine bourgeoisie (Madame Jourdain) and the genuine
aristocracy (Dorante) speak out in opposition to
Jourdain's illusions, the one voice speaking a proverb-
laden, plain and blunt language, the other a witty,
pleasing, and elegant one. These voices are intermingled in the play's musical score with other, partly serious, partly cheerful, partly natural, and also partly
caricatured voices.

The Would-Be Gentleman is one of Molière's most
colorful and entertaining comedies. It begins with a
four-part introduction, four "numbers," as it were, in
which Monsieur Jourdain's conceited transformation
from a bourgeois into a nobleman takes place. Dance,
music, fencing, and philosophy, that is, the fine arts of
a cultivated man are represented one after the other.
Jourdain has no particular inclinations for these arts;
he merely wishes to deck himself in these accomplishments as with borrowed plumes. On the other hand,
those people who have been engaged to teach him
their particular art merely fancy themselves as artists;
like almost all characters who represent professions in
Molière's works (as well as those of his predecessors),
they are basically pedants. The twofold ridiculousness
of these teachers and their pupil produces twofold
comedy.

In the first three "numbers" (dance, music, and
fencing), comedy is achieved primarily through gesture, by means of which Molière underscores the
teachers' pedantic seriousness and the pupil's awkward
and mechanical bungling. In the fourth number, the

comedy is achieved through language; the philosopher speaks an absurdly exaggerated professional jargon and the pupil, hypnotized by big words and platitudes, mechanically parrots the nonsense that he has been told. Jourdain's refrain in all four numbers is: "Is that what people of quality do?" He never asks: "Is it good?"

Jourdain is in no way changed by what he learns; he only masquerades with this learning. From time to time his genuinely bourgeois nature breaks through his pretenses; for example, this is absurdly apparent when he interrupts the music master's delicate chanson with a plain folk song (like Mascarille, Jourdain sings although he has not studied music). His "good sense" also breaks through the masquerade when he interrupts the philosopher's pedantic discourse on logical and ethical axioms. He remains a bourgeois in the eyes of his teachers, who are interested only in his money and not in developing his abilities.

Taken together the four numbers form a dramatic structure which can be termed choreographic: pas de deux, solos, corps de ballet with soloists—all providing a fluid succession of events, artistic variation, and the greatest stylization. The dialogue is also choreographically conceived in its rhythmic variation of short and long lines, its most subtly stylized prose, and its gesture-laden catchwords.

Molière adds a counterpoint in the third act. Madame Jourdain and Nicole, the maid, oppose their own good sense to the nonsense going on all around them. These two women represent two practical views concerning Monsieur Jourdain's mania and his vanity which seeks fulfillment in a social rank beyond his reach. First, we have the flatly realistic perspective of the bourgeois wife who continually and bluntly refers to her husband's permanent enthusiasm for his ridiculous occupations and accomplishments as "nonsense." Her refrain is: you should see to your household, make a suitable match for your daughter, and remain in your own trade; in a word, you should be what you are. Nicole's complementary perspective has its origin in the peasant and working classes. She reduces Monsieur Jourdain's feverish activity with teachers and aristocratic guests to the simple formula: more unnecessary work for me. Dancing, singing, fencing, good manners, and philosophy—all are nothing but *galimatias*, nonsense. Jourdain's attempts to produce counter-evidence, result in a shortened repetition of the four original numbers, repetition of the pseudo-philosophical nonsense concerning the distinctions between prose and verse, and a repetition of the fencing nonsense. However, since Jourdain is now opposing this nonsense to the good sense of the two women who seek to expose his folly, the comedy here differs from that seen at the beginning of the play when Jourdain's paid teachers applauded his efforts.

The heightening of the counterpoint and the beginning of the intrigue is facilitated by the figure of Dorante, a genuine nobleman and a modified Don Juan figure, at least insofar as his tactics for seduction and eluding his creditor are concerned. He exploits Jourdain's enthusiasm and voracious ambition for his own purposes. He concocts an amusing, but risky intrigue involving himself and his beloved Dorimène. Extract-

ing money from Jourdain for costly presents to Dorimène, he then presents them in his own name and not
on behalf of Jourdain, as he had promised to do in his
role of go-between. He arranges for a dinner for her
in Jourdain's house and provides some gratis entertainment "encouraging" the bourgeois's amorous grimaces. Dorante delights in the dialectical play of the
twofold misunderstandings, in his own dangerous
game, and in the airs Jourdain gives himself. For he,
too, wishes to teach Jourdain a lesson—"from above,"
as it were, just as Madame Jourdain wishes to do so
"from below."

In addition to this counterpoint, and attached to the
end of the intrigue, we find one of Molière's typical
secondary plots: the theme of thwarted young love.
Lucile Jourdain and Cléonte have pledged themselves
to one another, but her father's drive for a higher
social position threatens to separate these lovers forever. As usual, they must devise some kind of maneuver in which they appear to bend to the tyrant's will,
nourish his fancies, lull him into a sense of false se-
curity, and then hit hard when he least suspects it.
This time, the intrigue makes use of Jourdain's snobbishness and craze for titles. Cléonte is disguised as a
Turkish prince and introduced to the covetous bourgeois as a suitor for his daughter's hand. Jourdain
trades his daughter for a fantastic Turkish title and in
this way everyone is satisfied at the end. There is no
denouement and no gruesome awakening for the
dupe: everything is resolved cheefully in a dance.
Dorante and Dorimène, Lucile and Cléonte are
united; Nicole gets Covielle, Cléonte's servant who, in

his role as the play's Harlequin, had devised the Turkish escapade. The play ends when Jourdain, still madly
ecstatic over his supposed ennoblement, negates himself and says: "I give . . . my wife to anyone who will
have her." He is incurable to the end.

   In a colorful alternation on stage of the various par-
ticipating parties, the double intrigue is unraveled in a
succession of numbers, each of which illustrates some
interpersonal configuration, particular mood, or virtuoso performance. To begin with, there is the tête-à-
tête between Cléonte and Covielle in which Cléonte
wishes to have the latter exorcise his love for Lucile
by means of a Socratic game of question and answer.
An example of the highest art of dramatic choreog-
raphy can be seen in the quartet in which the two
girls, Lucile and Nicole, confront the two men,
Cléonte and Covielle. At first Cléonte is sulkily annoyed with Lucile, then they mince about and give
themselves airs, then Lucile is annoyed with Cléonte,
and finally the quarrel is settled to everyone's satisfac-
tion.

   There is also the trio consisting of Jourdain, Dorante, and Dorimène in which Dorante mediates between his lady and the bourgeois, who have no idea of
the real situation. He pours his catchwords first into
the one's ear and then into the other's, and like an able
helmsman, he sails around the dangerous reefs of mis-
understanding so skillfully that tension and laughter
result from the succeeding shocks. Finally, we have
the "Turkish" scene in which extravagant comical
effects stem from the double vision involved. (Jourdain
takes the ceremony seriously while everyone else, in-

cluding the audience, experiences it as a masquerade.) The grotesque-exotic ballet is combined with a grotesque-nonsensical play of words ("*galimatias à la turquie*") and the play becomes a "total" spectacle in which the theme of the "would-be gentleman" resounds fortissimo in full orchestration and fantastic exaggeration.

Louis XIV said afterward that Molière "had never created anything better than this." He had never made such good use of the theater's potential as he had in this comedy. Placing himself at a great distance from real life, he was able to illustrate one of life's truths in the lightest possible way. He had mounted a comedy in the idiom of the ballet which exposed the dynamic forces at work in society: its stable and reasonable representatives cheerfully embodied in the down-to-earth Madame Jourdain and Nicole; its decadents and libertines in the figures of Dorante and Dorimène; and its energetic and upwardly mobile members in Monsieur Jourdain.

The Mischievous Machinations
of Scapin
(Les Fourberies de Scapin, 1671)

　　　　Molière's troupe shared its theater in Paris
with "The Italians," a group of Italian players in the
commedia dell'arte tradition, headed by the legendary
Scaramouche. This situation created a healthy climate
of energetic competition and tug of war for the favor
of the public. For Molière as director, actor, and
playwright, the result of his association with the Italians, whose eminently lively theatrical technique ex-
celled in the area of mime and gesture, was constant
innovation in his own theatrical craft. The proximity
of the Italians also gave him an opportunity to try out
what he had produced. Thus, the constant mutual
contact (for years each troupe performed and ob-
served each other on alternate evenings) prevented the
troupe from falling into the routine and Molière from
creating drama that was more literary than theatrical.
　　The Italians were both a stimulation and an elixir of
life for the aging Molière, who in his last years was ill

and also disappointed in many areas of his life. They kept alive his ability to change so that his later plays preserved the same astonishing verve and vital tempo that had characterized his work from the very beginning. It was from the Italians and their French counterparts—(the comic players at country fairs, folk farce players, acrobats, and pranksters)—that Molière learned the fundamental principles of his craft. These players constantly reinforced Molière's belief in simplicity, dramatic stylization, concentration on the practical, quick tempo, and abundant gesture. From them he learned all of the theatrical tricks common to the folk theater, and designed to make people laugh.

He also learned from them all the traditional comic situations, characters, and plots of an ancient but oral theatrical tradition; in other words, he took from these folk players whatever he needed ("I take what belongs to me wherever I find it"), all those things which actually formed the foundation of his comedies. It is said that the actor Molière—whose style of acting we will, unfortunately, never be able to imagine perfectly, but who was considered to be the best comic actor of his day—learned a great deal by watching Scaramouche and Tabarin, the great French farce player. We can see this from the roles he played in his own comedies and which he had created specifically for himself. Moreover, the folk theater was never entirely banned even from the great and elegant comedies. The low comedy which often complements the higher form of comedy in such works is embodied in servants and peasant characters who performed the tricks (*lazzi*) found in the *commedia dell'arte*: the beatings and teasings of farce, and the grotesque gestures of the country fair pranksters.

In 1671, Molière was renovating his theater for the presentation of *Psyché*, a work of "total" theater whose fanciful whimsy was supported by splendid theatrical machinery and sets. However, he was in urgent need of a stand-by and wrote for this purpose *The Mischievous Machinations of Scapin*. People called it the Frenchman's curtsy to the *commedia dell'arte* (conceived as it was according to the principle of the thieving magpie, a method frequently imputed to Molière). *Scapin* was "pure theater," an archetypal entertainment in which jokes are played from beginning to end and in which there is no resemblance to reality, or at most, only accidental verisimilitude.

The play is *commedia dell'arte* in French and in prose. Scapin and the two elder burghers are masked characters. Its plot contains the familiar elements of obstructed love affairs, stubborn fathers, and cunning servants; it combines and makes use of disguises, confusions, dupings, and beatings—all in the quick tempo of slapstick comedy. Its dialogue is stylized in the direction of the absurd. In it the central intrigue has been thought out by one character who, like Till Eulenspiegel, Kasperle, or Harlequin, delights in playing tricks. He is a knave like Don Juan, but he does not swindle and defraud for the sake of money or self-interest or, indeed, to improve mankind; he does so for the pure pleasure of it.

Scapin is the unadulterated creation of a comedian's

fantasy, a theatrical figure who causes confusion and
re-establishes natural order in his small, artificially
constructed world. He is the quintessence of wit and
fanciful ideas, immune to fear and danger, a friend of
the weak and the simple, an opponent and terror of
the conceited and stupid. He is full of vitality, never
outwitted himself, at home in many roles, superior to
everyone, everywhere, everytime. No calculator and
planner, he improvises like a gambler whom fortune
always assists. Adventure is his whole life: "It amuses
me to tackle things where there is a little risk involved," he boasts. And again (Act I, Scene 2): "I've
quite a gift for smart ideas and ingenious little dodges.
Of course, those who can't appreciate them call'em
shady, but, boasting apart, there are not many fellows
equal to yours truly when it comes down to scheming
or something that needs a little manipulation."

Scapin's specialty is "to forge a machine." He is an
"engineer" in the terminology of his age. For this was
an age in which the latest Italian inventions and ingenious devices for the production of illusion and perspective were enthusiatically employed in all theatri-
cals celebrating court festivals. Scapin's "machines"
are constructions of his imagination. His "science"
consists in his knowledge of the weaknesses of those in
his environment, his desire for adventure, and his
humor. The individual parts of his machines are the
comedy's characters who are manipulated and played
against one another in such a way that they promptly
fall into every trap he sets them. The "machine"
works on behalf of the young and against the old, but
sometimes Scapin's insatiable delight in jest makes it

irresistible for him to play mild pranks even on the young people. However, he merely toys with these young people, but he snares and entraps their elders.

An expert in the art of tightrope walking over an abyss, nothing is too difficult for him. The more targets he has at one time, the better he likes it. He juggles six balls at once, simultaneously plays the servant to two masters (though, to be sure, unlike Goldoni's Harlequin, Scapin acts with the knowledge of both his masters), and executes almost identical missions for both of them. Duplication is an important structural principle of farce; episodic repetition with slight variation creates in these works both tension and comedy. Scapin sets the same traps for the old burghers Argante and Géronte, wraps both of them round his finger in the same manner, and manages to squeeze money out of them with similar ploys. Both these old men are misers, tyrants in their own homes, stubborn creatures cut from the same cloth as Harpagon and Argan; but they are two-dimensional figures designed in accordance with the style of farce, and they represent pure caricatures of their type. Their sons— Octave and Leander—are unimaginative weaklings. Both are in love with "unsuitable" girls, both are threatened with disinheritance, and both have been held on a tight rein by their intimidating fathers. They are traditional figures, the barest silhouettes of genuine young gallants, and the mere functions of Scapin's ingenuity. Their girl friends are the very picture of touching, unformed femininity, the one scarcely differentiated from the other. However, Zerbinette, the pseudo-gypsy girl, reveals an irrepressible loquacity, which aids the progression of the play; for through Zerbinette, Scapin's pranks become public and he nearly fails. Zerbinette's loquaciousness gives rise to the situation in which Scapin plays his last, most enormous prank: his feigned act of dying.

Adhering to a good old custom, Scapin creates fictional characters who, together with the available real ones, keep his intrigues against Argante and Géronte going. He does this through dissimulation and disguises (for example, Octave's servant Silvestre must pretend to be Zerbinette's sword-swinging soldier brother). Scapin's forte is acting, and we might well ask what he really is? He is the archetype of the mime who changes his identity as often as he likes, who can adopt several identities at once, or who "divides" himself, since he is driven by a superabundance of imagination into successively trying out several personalities. With Octave he rehearses a confrontation scene with an angry father; he also has a tryout with Silvestre. He presents himself as a contrite man when Leander angrily accuses him of having betrayed his love affairs; he presents himself as helpful to the fathers when in reality he is intent on wresting money from them to pay for their sons' escapades.

He multiplies himself for his most cruel and primitive prank. In order to vigorously repay Géronte for the particular difficulty which the latter's avariciousness and tenacity have caused him in the course of his swindle, Scapin tricks the old man into getting into a sack. (The sack, now a symbol for Scapin, was a prop which Molière took from the Grand Guignol and Brighella.) Once Géronte is in the sack, Scapin thrashes him to his heart's content while at the same time disguising his voice in such a way as to make Géronte think that the empty stage is really populated with an entire company of hearty soldiers. Caught out in the middle of his best swing—Géronte is not quite so stupid—Scapin just about manages to get away. The prank fails because Scapin has allowed himself to be carried away by his own ideas.

For Scapin is not a model of caution. He often carries things to a point where they become dangerous. However, the more risky the situation becomes, the better he thinks, and the more tense and exciting the play becomes. He trusts in chance, or rather, the author employs chance so subtly as a structural element of his play that the action seems to develop in a constant and seamless progression; the plot is consciously artificial, but so artistically realized that the spectator is given no opportunity to doubt the plausibility of events on stage. Chance causes to cross Scapin's path the very person he needs to further his various parallel deceptions. There is a constant coming and going on the stage; everything is speeded up in the style of farce; and the situations are first confused and then disentangled in the most complicated manner so that the spectator has some difficulty in separating the individual threads of the net.

The climax of the fraud is reached in the scene with Géronte. In order to fleece him of 500 écus, Scapin concocts a highly ornate story about a Turk who has abducted Géronte's son and is holding him prisoner in his galley. (The play takes place in Naples, the heartland of the *commedia dell'arte*.) This lie, improvised on the spot, becomes more and more colorful and exotic when Géronte maintains his stiff resistance. On the one hand, his devotion to his son forces him to deliver up the money; on the other hand, he is too exhausted to resist the nimble-witted Scapin, who never lacks for an "ingenious" answer to one of his questions.

The mobility of this scene, its wealth of gesture and dialogue makes it the climax of the play. It is a virtuoso piece of the comic muse in which agility is played off against rigidity, pure ingenuity against unimaginativeness. Scapin has completed his most difficult task by using all of his various talents: role-playing, storytelling, skillful argumentation, artful improvisation, and—most of all—his knowledge of human nature. (These are, of course, Molière's talents.) In Scapin, we see the engineer at work with an elegance and lightness which are reminiscent of Don Juan, the aristocratic Proteus in Molière's gallery of impostors.

In this comedy, which has neither theme nor moral nor satirical intention, and with this figure of Scapin, who is motivated by nothing but the joy of playing games with people, Molière devoted himself totally to his craft as a playwright. In wild exuberance, he pulled all of the stops on the instrument of his comic muse. This servant of two masters serves comedy alone. Like his dramatic predecessor, the slave in Roman comedy, he allows himself to be hired. He does this in order to execute his masters' "rascally" business. But in final analysis he surrenders himself not to his masters but only to comedy—and he does so body and soul.

The conclusion of the play is as fantastic as the characters who take part in it. There is a general shuffling of identities from which the two girls emerge as socially acceptable brides for the two young men. The two fathers also get back their two lost daughters. Thus Scapin's pranks produce the wished-for results. But because he has played one prank too many (the "small" act of revenge on Géronte) he must be called to account for his actions. Desperately, but not hopelessly, he allows his best prank to take shape in his mind. He mimes the role of a grievously wounded man and has himself carried on stage on a stretcher in the midst of a scene of general reconciliation and rejoicing. Here he appeals "in the presence of death" to the compassion and tender-heartedness of his justly angered opponents.

As realistically as ever, Scapin plays the role of the contrite, suffering, repentant sinner and imposes his wretchedness on those who try to ward him off. Glad to be able to show generosity, they are also impatient to be rid of Scapin once and for all. Thus they quickly absolve him of his deeds, but when they suspect that they have once again fallen into a trap, they reconsider their graciousness. As Géronte says: "I only forgive you on condition that you die. (. . . .) If you get better, I withdraw my forgiveness." However, the general joy is too great, the cheerful mood produced by the miraculous solution is too contagious, and Scapin is once again irresistible—in any case, the joke of the play as a whole must have a comical end. Thus Scapin must once again get off scot-free and have the last amusing word. As everyone is preparing for a banquet, Scapin tells them "to carry me to the foot of the table and I'll wait there till death comes to claim me."

The Learned Women
(Les Femmes savantes, 1672)

This play is the last of the series of great and elegant comedies. More classical and purer in form than the others, it has greater regularity in structure and subtlety in composition. It is woven of three themes: learned women, the contemporary world of letters, and bourgeois marital conflict. Molière recalled the themes of his first Parisian success, *The Precious Damsels*, but adapted them to the somewhat changed times: precious snobs became learned women; people read philosophers instead of romantic novels; farce was transposed into great comedy; the main characters were given a precise psychological profile; and instead of prose, Molière used somewhat over-lofty Alexandrine verse. Many critics have found fault with this play because of its slow pace and lengthy discussions.

The *dramatis personae* is long and judiciously balanced. The three learned women—the mother, sister-in-law, and daughter—are each precisely differentiated

characters who represent progressive studies in ridiculous feminine erudition. They stand in opposition to
the "natural" men: Chrysale (father, husband, and
head of the house), Clitandre (the suitor), and Ariste
(Chrysale's brother and the play's "rascal"). The un-
learned daughter, Henriette, moves between these
groups as a connecting link, and the stumbling block is
provided by the aesthete Trissotin. An impostor like
Tartuffe, he is considerably more harmless, but he is as
ridiculous as Oronte in *The Misanthrope* and Mascarille in *The Precious Damsels*. Like Oronte and Mascarille, Trissotin has a scene in which a sonnet is read
aloud; like Tartuffe, he is unscrupulously ambitious, a
fortune hunter and a hypnotic personality; however,
he affects only those who are "conceited."

The conflict takes place between those who are
learned and those who are natural, between genuine
and arrogated authority, between rigidity and flexibility. The tension builds up to an explosion catalyzed by
Trissotin; the battlefronts become clearly defined, and
the various characters reveal themselves to be either
genuine human beings or merely masked figures. For
Trissotin, the existence of Philaminte, Bélise, and Armande is contrary to reason and to life. For them,
being a woman is a matter of personifying aestheticism, of courtly games of love. They share with the
precious snobs of the earlier play the same horror of
the physical and the natural. They consider themselves
clever when they opt for the intellect, for form instead of substance. However, what these ridiculous
learned ladies understand by intellect is parrot-like
repetition, enumeration of facts, ecstatic agreement

with one another; they are incapable of making independent judgments or engaging in independent reflection. This is illustrated in the scene in which Trissotin's sonnet is read aloud and all three rapturously admire his trivial words. It is further demonstrated by their enthusiastic reception of Vadius when they learn that he knows Greek. They judge by the letter and not by the worth of a person or his talent. Their erudition is as superficial here as the preciosity in the earlier work; it is a woman's escape into fantasy from the unpleasant role she must play in opposition to a man. A legitimate protest has assumed false forms.

Psychological cracks may be seen in the masks of the two unmarried women. Bélise in particular reveals the symptoms of a frustrated woman (like the prudish Arsinoé in *The Misanthrope*). She sees a suitor in disguise in every man, especially when he rebuffs her. Armande, the false philosopher, is still very much interested in love (but love of a gallant sort) and is piqued by the fact that Clitandre, weary of her coyness, has turned to her sister Henriette. She had considered the man as her possession, as a plaything of her moods and her pride. Thus it did not occur to her that he could prefer Henriette's devotion and true femininity to her own glittering intellectuality. For Armande, Henriette's advantages are seen as negative, as are also marriage, sex, and bourgeois domesticity.

Molière illustrates Armande's and Madame Philaminte's contempt for conventional men by introducing Chrysale. Chrysale represents quite a different kind of bourgeois; he is softer, relatively more flexible, and more reasonable. While wishing to adhere to the

time-honored traditional rules for governing his bourgeois household, he is no tryant. He is concerned with
his comfort and with the smooth functioning of his
household and his family life. In contrast to Arnolphe,
Argan, Orgon, and Harpagon, however, he does not
have a very secure grip on the reigns of authority. His
wife wears the pants in his house; it is she who scolds
the servants, undertakes to marry off her daughters,
and sets the tone of family life. In *her* house, not even
the humblest maid is allowed to contravene the rules
of grammar; in *his* house, however, the kitchen must
be good, that is, the body must be at least as well
nourished as the mind. For Chrysale, the cook who
allows her roast to burn because she is absorbed in a
novel is neither a woman nor a servant. He dreams of
the gentle girls of his gallant past, but his household is
full of recalcitrant women who challenge his authority
and who continually seek to undermine his concepts
of a reasonable way of life with their pedantry and
affectations of culture. He makes only weak attempts
to break this rule of women. Against his protests, Philaminte dismisses the maid Martine because her vowels
and her grammar are not "correct." This incident
shows that Chrysale has not been master of his own
house for quite a while.

Does concession in small things lead to concession in
important matters? The present issue is Henriette's
marriage. Will she be permitted to take the suitor of
her own choice, a man approved of by Chrysale? Or
must she accept Trissotin, who has won the heart of
her mother and the other learned women by means of
his insipid, modish verses, his flatteries, and his obei-

sances? Is it to be a natural or an unnatural marriage? Shall the authority rest with the husband or with the wife, that is, with the man or with the women? Philaminte dislikes Clitandre because he has never asked if he might read something aloud to her; that is, she dislikes him because he is honest. She believes that through Trissotin, she can insure her rebellious daughter's education as a *femme savante* (a learned woman). Her small domestic world is to be ordered according to her own concepts and not according to the preferences and requirements of her daughters or her husband.

Chrysale possesses tolerance but lacks will power. Like all Molière's bourgeois figures, he becomes irritable when he should remain firm. At one point he appears destined to lose again. At best, it would seem that the conflict between Philaminte and Chrysale will result in a checkmate. However, Ariste, the *raisonneur* brother, brings about the miraculous and poetic turn of events which insures that everything comes out satisfactorily. Trissotin is unmasked as an impostor and a fortune hunter; Clitandre is shown to be the genuine suitor who deserves to win Henriette.

The lines between the tender and the hard people are precisely drawn. On the one side, there are those for whom preference, sincerity, natural authority, and the equilibrium of life forces decide the issue; on the other side, there are those who wish to force and manipulate people, who give their full praise to trivial and inessential things, and who consider their opinions infallible. But Ariste's maneuver functions as a *deus ex machina*. It obstructs Trissotin's plans and allows a different face to appear from behind the proferred mask: Philaminte's stoicism, heretofore mere talk, is validated during a scene in which she is—incorrectly —informed that Chrysale has been bankrupted. Accepting the catastrophe with philosophic equanimity, she expects the same attitude from others, especially Trissotin, but she does so in vain. Armande's sour face over this sudden change in fortune, which will surely diminish her chances of marriage, bespeaks her repressed womanliness. Henriette's generosity in refusing to drag Clitandre down with her in the family's misfortunes touchingly rounds out the portrait of an engaging personality. In this skillfully manipulated moment of truth, everyone is tested and found to be either genuine or false. Each shows himself for what he is: Bélise as imprisoned forever in her fantasy world; Chrysale as reliant upon outside help because of his weakness of character; his wife as the family's genuine authority emerges essentially undamaged from the labyrinth of misunderstood aestheticism and does the right thing.

Into this conflict-laden plot about obstructed love and confusion of authority, Molière has skillfully, but perhaps somewhat long-windedly, woven a wealth of reflections upon the play's three themes. More than any of his other works, *The Learned Women* becomes a discussion play (and a treasury of quotations for later generations). It is also a comedy of manners rich in ideas. Moreover, in one famous scene, the play indulges in contemporary polemics. Trissotin's poems are genuine examples from the pen of one Abbé Cotin, one of Molière's open opponents. Trissotin is a

somewhat sinister caricature of Cotin, whose own famous debate with a literary rival called Ménage is
reproduced in a ridiculously intensified form in the
confrontation between Trissotin and Vadius. Molière's portrait of Trissotin as a hardhearted impostor
—eager to force into marriage a young girl whom he
jilts when he learns that her dowry is lost—is a private
act of revenge within the permissible limits of poetic
freedom. It is, perhaps, a bit severe but extremely
effective dramaturgy.

With respect to his fraudulent relationship to Henriette, Trissotin resembles Tartuffe. However, since
he has already been made into such a ridiculous figure
long before the end of the play (in the poetry reading
scene and in his dispute with Vadius), he appears a less
frightening imposter than his powerful and wicked
predecessor. The combined representatives of goodness opposing Trissotin are more massive and more
inventive than Tartuffe's touching but helpless opponents, all of whom are totally reliant on Elmire's resoluteness. In *The Learned Women*, the impostor is
opposed by upright masculinity as well as by an un-
perturbable and steadfast feminine character. When he
is unmasked, he neither wishes nor is able to undertake
a counteraction. The representatives of goodness do
not have to be saved by outside intervention; they
help themselves. Society is intact; before irreparable
damage is done it removes from its midst a malignant
foreign body.

Does Molière once again show a greater measure of
belief in society and in the triumph of its inherent
humanity? One might be tempted to think so. How-

ever, when compared with the more dynamic earlier play, *The Learned Women* reveals a rather academic bloodlessness, especially in its artful though somewhat ponderous verse dialogue. We know that when Molière wrote this play, he was quite ill, that he was not happy in his domestic life, and that he was oppressed by opponents on all sides. Did he thus wish to design a counterpart to the world which he himself had experienced, a more cheerful and more equable world?

The Imaginary Invalid
(Le Malade imaginaire, 1673)

  Molière's last play offers the best commentary on the much discussed autobiographical aspects of his work: the mortally ill dramatist wrote a comedy about an imaginary invalid, himself portrayed this man on the stage, and at one point allowed him to feign death, asking beforehand: "Isn't there some danger in pretending to be dead?" He lets him enter into a discussion with his brother on the subject of himself (Molière) and say to him, among other things, that if he (Argan) were a doctor and knew that Molière were ill, he would allow him to die as a punishment for his constant attacks against doctors in his comedies. To this, his brother (Béralde) responds that Molière was not portraying medicine itself but only "the absurdities of medicine." In other words, his target is those doctors who convert imaginary invalids into truly sick people, doctors who should be allowed to treat only robust people capable of triumphing over the ridiculous cures they are subjected to. He (Molière) would be happy, however, if they would leave him alone since he has only just about enough strength "to bear his illness."

That this was no vain exaggeration was to be proved at the fourth performance of this play, when Argan-Molière had an attack of faintness in the middle of the concluding ballet just as he had to speak the word *juro* during the conferral of his medical degree. Concealing this attack behind a grimace, he managed with the greatest effort to keep going for the few remaining minutes of the play, and died at home later that night.

What a marvelous writer of comedy Molière was—a man able to laugh at himself despite the most difficult personal circumstances: professional annoyance (his colleague Lully had outdone him in obtaining the King's favor); misery at home (a son had died one month after birth, his wife lived apart from him for all practical purposes, his old girl friend and professional comrade Madeleine Béjart had recently died); severe illness, probably tuberculosis augmented by the total exhaustion caused by years of overwork; and finally, the knowledge that he did not have much longer to live. And yet, he understood how to turn his autobiography upside down. A truly ill man, he wrote for himself the role of a would-be invalid; as a dramatist and actor, he projected a mirror image of himself, excluding every trace of self-pity and existential anxiety. In other words, he transformed unpleasant personal reality into a multi-reflected drama which was nourished by experience, but in which experience was so objectified and distilled that it could be traced to its original roots only in a roundabout way.

The theme lay close to Molière's heart and the role corresponded to his physical fragility. But in order to make something theatrical out of all of this, as he conceived of the theater and had written for it up till now, he reversed his outward symptoms and even employed the illusion-shattering comical trick of letting himself become the object of discussion. Having heaped the curses of doctors on his own head, Molière pronounced his own death sentence. He was an artist and a comedian to the last, even in the presence of death.

The Imaginary Invalid was another ballet-comedy (or as it was called this time, a comedy with music and dance). However, Lully did not compose the music for this work, as he had done for many of the previous comedies. The two had quarreled and the Florentine had maneuvered Molière out of his exclusive position at court. Thus, although it was written to celebrate France's recent victories in Holland, the play was not premiered at court but rather in Paris, at Molière's own theater. For the last time Molière displayed his multiple talents as the "King of Laughter" and wrote one of his most famous and most enduringly popular plays before making his final exit.

He had long been familiar with the play's main theme—the ridiculous aspects of medicine—having devoted an entire farce to it (*The Doctor in Spite of Himself*), and many times employed it as a secondary theme. While the grotesque *commedia dell'arte* doctor is not really a character in Molière's works, he became one of the most important catalyzing agents in his comic world. For this figure's sphere of action is precisely that area in which Molière's contemporaries most markedly paraded their gullibility and stupidity. The seventeenth century was a dark and obscurantist century insofar as medicine was concerned. Doctors treated and cured haphazardly, following Hippocrates in a totally blind manner. In diagnosing, they relied on wild hypothesis. Anatomy was still in its infancy and new discoveries (such as Harvey's discovery of blood circulation) were considered inconvenient heresies by the majority of doctors.

Chronic conservatives, like all specialists who enjoy great social prestige, doctors have always had the reputation of being arrogant, fanatical, and dogmatic. In Molière's century, they had achieved a high social rank, though not precisely on the basis of their expertise. Their influence at court was both great and notorious. The royal family in particular had suffered a great deal at their hands. That Louis XIV enjoyed excellent health was proved by the fact that he lived to an old age, fairly undamaged by the infinite bleedings prescribed by zealous and ignorant doctors. Molière's belief that doctors should only treat robust people found confirmation in the King himself. The Queen was less fortunate: four of her children died shortly after birth, and she herself died young, having been criminally mistreated by doctors.

As a patient of long standing, Molière had ample opportunity to observe his doctors closely (his illness was described as a *fluxion*, but he probably suffered from tuberculosis of the lungs). He therefore came to the conclusion that the art of medicine generally did the patient more harm than good, that the doctors

played a game of hocus-pocus in prescribing medicines, since they were not in a position to explain the
connection between a disease and its supposed remedy.
In addition, then as now, there were fashions and obsessions in medicine. It was not yet a scientific dis-
cipline, but rather a profession—like that of priests
—in which faith played the most important role.
Moreover, medicine corresponded to the church in
other ways, including the necessity for the doctor to
fit himself into a similar hierarchy.

The apothecary in *The Imaginary Invalid* appeals to
the *"ordonnances de la médicine"* when Argan tries to
postpone his enema at the insistence of his brother
Béralde. *"Ordonnance"* means more here than the
specific word "prescription." It contains a strong con-
notation of the word "commandment." Argan's doctor, Monsieur Purgon, whom the apothecary has hur-
riedly sent for, is greatly excited by this "rebellion of
a patient against his doctor," that is to say, by the
crime of *"lèse-faculté"* (treason against the Faculty
of Medicine).

Purgon treats and punishes Argan just as a priest
would a sinner; he will have nothing more to do with
his disobedient patient and casts him out as an unbe-
liever. He delivers him up to his bad constitution and
utters a curse which, within four days, is supposed to
reduce Argan to an incurable state of health. Argan
thereupon gives himself up for dead, since he has blind
faith in doctors. He accepts medicine's punishment as
obediently as he had previously accepted its smallest
commandments. Béralde sagaciously characterizes the
command-obedience relationship between doctor and

patient: "It seems, to hear you, that Monsieur Purgon holds the thread of your days in his hands, and that by supreme authority he lengthens it and shortens it as he pleases."

Molière demonstrates the absurd nature of blind belief in authority by choosing an imaginary invalid rather than a genuine one. Argan suffers the anxiety of a dogmatic believer convinced that his only salvation lies in following instructions to the letter. He therefore becomes mortally confused when he forgets the doctor's exact instructions. ("Monsieur Purgon told me to take a walk in my room in the morning, twelve times up and back; but I forgot to ask him whether he meant lengthwise or crosswise.") A timid subordinate, his obedience to commands has become a matter of the strictest ritual, rather than one of reason or necessity.

This is established by an introductory monologue in which Argan calculates the seriousness of his illness according to the number of individual treatments he has undergone. A month in which he has taken fewer medicines and fewer enemas is consequently a "bad" month, and he decides to ask Monsieur Purgon to give him more of both in order to set matters right again. Like a true bourgeois, when Argan makes his calculations, measuring the doctor's bill against the treatment received, he is thinking not of the state of his health but only of the state of his purse. He is interested not in a cure but in the financial possibility of continuing to be sick. Monsieur Purgon's fees are accepted as reasonable, but not those of the apothecary, who sits lower in the hierarchy: "Ah, Monsieur Fleurant, gently, if you please; if you treat people like that, they won't want to be sick any more." Without intending to do so, he has let the cat out of the bag: he is pretending to be sick as a pleasurable activity, a kind of hobby.

The typical bourgeois concern with one's body has become in Argan's case a not unpleasant obsession in which he invests his money and for which he unhesitatingly sacrifices his daughter. This obsession has also made him blind to the hypocrisy of his wife as long as she plays along with him and pretends to take his "hobby" seriously. Molière has skillfully placed this aspect of Argan's conceit at the beginning of the play; here, he reads the apothecary's bill and first of all expresses pleasure at the fact that it has been so "politely" worded. "What I like about Monsieur Fleurant, my apothecary, is that his bills are always very civil," he says. Secondly, he is as ecstatically absorbed and enraptured by the sound of the exotic medical terminology enumerated in the bill as a miser is at the sight and sound of his money. The only thing he demands of those authorities he has set above him is that they allow him to persevere in his illness in a "reasonable" way. He is vexed with Fleurant because the latter has overestimated the state of his pocketbook. He considers Fleurant's demands for money a mockery and tells him that he must learn to live with his patients. As long as the doctors remain within these limits, Argan gives them dog-like obedience. This corresponds to his concept of reason.

Toinette, the rebellious maid and Angélique's ally, disguises herself as a doctor and comes to take a look, as she says, at this "famous invalid." In so doing, she impels the play towards the moment of truth by means of the comic exposure appropriate to comedy; she brings about a situation in which Argan's credulity reaches its limits. Toinette recommends the amputation of one arm and the removal of an eye (an allusion to the Bible: the "afflicted" eye, the "afflicted" arm). Argan is perplexed. This logical extension of the treatments his own doctors have applied in a somewhat milder form finally strikes home. It would no longer be a pleasure to be sick. "Cut off one of my arms, and put out one of my eyes, so that the other one will be healthier? I'd much rather it wasn't so healthy," he says in agitation.

But he still does not notice that there is something not quite right about medicine as a whole—nor will he ever. His thought processes and self-centeredness enable him to hold on to his obsession to the very end. This is so despite the fact that the doctor's curses do not come true and that the hypocrisy of Béline's interest in his illness is revealed when he feigns death.

Argan does the most logical things from his own point of view (although they are really the most absurd), and therefore allows himself to play a double role: the commander and the obedient subordinate. Béralde, the reasonable brother, has realized that his whimsical brother cannot be cured of his obsession. The best that he can do is to isolate Argan so that he can harm no one but himself. (Angélique has again escaped by the skin of her teeth.) He wants to have a doctor in the family? Then it is best that he become one himself. How does one become a doctor? Molière says—along with Argan and Béralde—in the simplifying language of comedy: all one needs is the doctor's cap and gown. Argan: "What? A man knows how to discourse upon illnesses when he has that costume?" Béralde: "Yes. One has only to talk with a cap and gown on. Any gibberish becomes learned, and any nonsense becomes reason."

Molière has expressed a hard truth in the language of comedy. Argan's graduation to the rank of doctor takes place in the form of a grotesque ballet, pure entertainment. His own delight becomes the audience's delight. By transforming the medical degree ceremony into a grotesque-fantastic dance pantomime, Molière expresses his most caustic opinion on the matter at hand—as he had done once before in *The Would-Be Gentleman* when Monsieur Jourdain was ennobled in the course of the Turkish masquerade. All of medicine is laughable, it is nothing but a masquerade.

Argan is more than an imaginary invalid who has focused his egotism upon his own body in a more perverted and more extreme manner than Chrysale in *The Learned Women*. He is also a tyrannical father and head of the house with a predilection for impostors. (In this he is like Orgon in *Tartuffe* or Philaminte in *The Learned Women*.) He must first learn to see through deception before its tyranny can be broken (the parallels to *Tartuffe* continue). Everyone else knows what Argan cannot admit to himself because he has completely identified with his obsession: namely, that he is in reality absolutely healthy and even, as Toinette says, basically a good man. Deceived by appearances, he is his own fool and the fool of others. His illness is as real for him as is the humbug with which the doctors and the apothecary take him in; it is also as real as the hypocritical love which his wife Béline shows him, and as real as his absurd "graduation."

He sacrifices all his bourgeois virtues to appearances. He violates his healthy concern for the family by planning to marry his daughter to a silly medical student in order to save money by procuring a doctor as a son-in-law. He sins against the reasonable upbringing of his children when he forces his little daughter Louison to spy on her sister's love affairs. He contravenes good sense with his gullibility and his admiration for nonsense, and he injures humanity in general with his total self-centeredness and lack of consideration for the happiness of others.

He is the quintessential comic character of Molière's comedies. He deserves to be punished and to become the butt of laughter and mockery. He is betrayed on all sides by those out to feather their own nests. For example, Angélique joins an alliance with Toinette, her lover Cléante, and Argan's reasonable brother Béralde. This alliance is established to prevent the absurd marriage between Angélique and Doctor Diafoirus's semi-idiotic son Thomas. The doctors, too, conspire together. Only Béline plays her deceitful game alone. In addition to the ridiculous, wicked impostors, there are those who intrigue in self-defense: Cléante smuggles himself into Argan's house as a music teacher in order to be near Angélique and to save her. His declaration of love is an improvised duet (we must remember that the play is a ballet-comedy);

Béralde's outwitting of Argan is the last of a series of such duperies (presented as a pantomime).

The "legitimate" intriguer Toinette effervesces with a wealth of ingenuity. Like the maid Dorine in *Tartuffe*, she possesses a truly ferocious loyalty to her mistress Angélique. Her resoluteness and glibness make her into an opponent equal to Argan, whose quarrels with Toinette are as pleasurable to him as is his imaginary illness (Act I, Scene 4). Argan: "What! I won't even have the pleasure of scolding her?" Toinette: "Scold me, have your fill of it, I'm willing." Argan: "But you stop me, you wench, by interrupting at every turn."

Toinette plays the role of the fraudulent doctor who carries "medicine" to the point of an absurdity. She lends her powers and her tongue to each maneuver undertaken to expose fraudulence: the unmasking of Madame Béline and the concluding masquerade really suit her admirably. Preserving her loyalty to the end, as a reasonable daughter of the people she rebels against the presumptions and infringements of the conceited bourgeois. Instinct and native wit make her into one of the most cheerful and vigorous characters in this multi-faceted play.

Like all Molière's young lovers, Angélique and Cléante are presented as still unformed and innocent. Angélique's filial obedience is first put to an extremely severe test when Argan speaks of marriage. Assuming that he has Cléante in mind, she quickly gives her father her assent and assures him of her blind obedience to him. Argan, however, has the doctor's son in mind and has totally neglected his duty as a father in favor of selfish (and therefore, to him, reasonable) choice of a suitor. She is tested a second time and maintains her filial loyalty even though she has passed through the fire of her father's tyranny and has long since given up hope of ever seeing her wishes fulfilled: Argan has feigned death in order to test his wife's love; Béline lets her mask fall and reveals the face of a hypocrite, while Angélique, another Cordelia, reveals herself to be all love and resignation. This is somewhat romantic, but it shows her strong character.

One could more easily see Angélique as the daughter of Béralde. As the play's *raisonneur*, he once again takes up the typical middle position. He mediates during the intrigues, comments upon the main theme, creates the "entertainment" both between the acts and at the end of the play, supports the voice of nature (as opposed to that of medicine), and speaks out for the rights of the young people to independence and free choice.

He is the counterbalance to all of the conceited, self-deluded characters in the play: to Argan as well as to the grotesquely exaggerated doctors who turn up in threes, the one more comical than the other—the impressive Monsieur Purgon, the sophistic Monsieur Diafoirus, and the literal-minded, ambitious Thomas Diafoirus. The appearance of the latter two has been worked into the second act with particular care. Father and son represent a caricatured portrait of command and obedience: shining examples of stupid conceit and conceited stupidity. The parrot-like babbling of the son, prompted by his father and constantly seeking his approval, is outdone by the father's speech in praise of his son: "For the rest, as regards the qualities requisite for marriage and propagation, I assure you that, according to the rules of our doctors, he is just as one could wish."

Only Molière's strict dramatic control prevents our tears from falling, for the grotesque contains elements of utmost seriousness. That comedy is one artistic possibility through which man can overcome his deepest suffering is here once again demonstrated. In this play, Molière emphasized the "artistic" aspect of his craft more than he had previously done, and continually adhered to the theatrical metaphor. Many of the most important episodes are conceived as "entertainment," the play breaks off into a ballet in order that a sad chapter may be concluded on a cheerful note. The borderland between life and death teems with impostors as well as with conceited and dangerous men. Let he who can, beware: Molière himself was not able to.

MOLIÈRE ON
THE CONTEMPORARY STAGE

The following excerpts from theatrical criticism of Molière's works are presented not with the idea of offering a complete picture but rather as a mosaic. There are many ways of interpreting Molière —including some that are mutually exclusive.

Georges Dandin
Deutsches Theater (1912)
Max Reinhardt, Director

Reinhardt places a genuinely suffering human being in an environment in which those about him either laugh at or trifle with suffering. He conjures up a powerful glow reminiscent of the brilliance of bygone days. "Nothing but love, love, love" is the leitmotif continually sung by these happy shepherds and shepherdesses. They dance through a rococo park, now sunny, now seductively dark in which kisses can be heard like the twittering of nightingales. Suffering from imaginary griefs, they skip over the beautifully curved sandstone edge of a pool of carp from which they must eventually be fished out with strong nets, but in which life is evidently possible for a few hours for a higher class of vertebrates. One quickly notes what the production is aiming for: an atmosphere laden with fantasy, boxes of toys, dallying, ballet, porcelain melancholy pierrots, contrasts of boorishness, the squeak of flutes and the sentimentality of the spinet, Lully, Louis XIV, illusion that is never supposed to achieve reality and yet does reach it here by means of a connecting link. The flightiness of an aristocracy—whose exuberant but superficial joy in living would be neither dampened nor made more profound were it to suspect how it would fare one hundred and twenty years later—felt itself attracted to the airiness of this pastoral way of life whose representatives bore such unreal names as Tirsio, Philen, Cloris, and Climene. The playwright and the director are in agreement as to their portrait of this social class: for it possesses no intrinsic life of its own, leading, rather, a marionette-like existence. It performs its ceremonial greetings to musical beats, depends in every way upon the emptiest of formalities, and pays for its newly fashionable palaces with the money of the peasant, whom it thanks with contempt and mistreatment. Here we come to the tragic aspect of this play. This Dandin would never have been a peasant even if he had been dressed in peasant clothing. However, he was and remains a human being. Sometimes he elicits our compassion, sometimes our horror; but he never creates a sense of cheerfulness in the spectator. . . .

Siegfried Jacobsohn, *Jahre der Bühne*, 1912.

Don Juan
Berlin Ensemble (1952)
Benno Besson, Director

Old works have their own values, their own
nuances, and their own scale of beauty and truth. It is
up to us to discover them. This does not mean that
Molière should be played now as he was played one
hundred seventy times before; it merely means that
one should not perform his works as they were performed in 1850 (and again in 1950). It is precisely the
manifold nature of perception and beauty which Molière's works reveal that allows us to draw from them
responses which are appropriate to our own age. Molière's *Don Juan* is of more value to us in its earlier
version than in the later one (which is also old). We
get more from the satire (which was also closer to
Molière himself) than from the quasi-tragic character
study. The brilliance of the parasite interests us less
than the parasitical nature of its brilliance. Philosophy
students of Leipzig University, discussing Besson's
production, found the satire on the feudal conception
of love as a hunt still so topical that they commented
with much laughter on the heartbreakers of today. . . .
Actually, Benno Besson's production of *Don Juan*
has twofold significance. First, he restored the comic
aspect of the Don Juan figure—which, incidentally, is
justified by Molière's original casting of the comedian

who usually played the comical Marquises in the role of Don Juan. Besson achieved this by simultaneously restoring the play's socio-critical statements. In the famous beggar scene, which heretofore had been used to show Don Juan as a freethinker and thus a progressive type, Besson presented only a libertine who was too arrogant to recognize any kind of obligations. This revealed how the ruling clique treated with indifference even that very religion which had been licensed and ordered by the State. Formally, Besson emancipated himself somewhat by doing away with the division of the play into five acts, a time-bound formalism. In carrying out this easy operation, he undoubtedly increased the public's amusement without sacrificing any of the play's meaning. What was also of significance for the German stage, was that Besson really understood how to make use of the invaluable tradition of the French theater. Amused, the public perceived the broad universal *niveau* of Molière's comedy, that daring mixture of the subtlest chamber-music comedy with the greatest farce, and here and there those small, delightfully serious passages unequaled anywhere.

Bertholt Brecht, *Plays*, Volume XII, 1962

Don Juan
Théâtre National Populaire (1956)
Jean Vilar, Director

Jean Vilar's *Don Juan* is a clown. He does not challenge us for a second. We find it delightful when he plays the double seducer with a buxom peasant girl on each arm; we find it captivating when he makes a fool of his creditor with his blarney phrased in terms of perfect politeness. In this way, he allows the various facets of this figure to come to light; indeed, he isolates these facets and parades them like the numbers of a musical comedy. He continually starts up a different engine, now it is that of seduction, then that of a joke, or of sarcasm, or cynicism.

The figure is never all of these things at once. In the last scene with Donna Elvire, his jilted wife, he allows himself to kneel before the melodically lamenting woman. But this act does not represent the paroxysm of mockery which Molière wished to illustrate here, the seducer's monstrous idea of daring to desire this humiliated woman once again in all her misery (in order to be able to reject her once again, as everyone knew). This action is both gallant and funny, a little blasé and a little bored. This is in keeping with Vilar's initial conception of the Don Juan figure, who drags himself along and is only propelled into action when he himself comes to some kind of a decision. Don

Juan's movements are strictly measured and he holds his gestures in tight rein; he has a tendency to lean on anything, preferably on his servant's shoulder, which functions like the wing of an armchair. Juan's basic attitude of weary arrogance, which is somewhat reminiscent of cant, is reflected in his voice: a wonderful voice in which the lyrical tones of an organ are intermingled with the sounds of heroic exaltation, the voice of a born actor in which Don Juan's blaséness streams forth complaisantly. But it is also a voice which requires only a little pressure in order to put itself at the service of his intelligence or powers of seduction. Vilar possesses *esprit*, but he does not embody it. Vilar masters the art of seduction, but he is no seducer. This Don Juan feels most satisfied when he is allowed to be a clown. Instead of seeking to honor the reputation of his name, he has only witticisms and jokes in mind with which he conceals from the audience his own inner vacuum.

Siegfried Melchinger, in *Modernes Welttheater*, 1956

Georges Dandin
Théâtre de la Cité de Villeurbanne (1962)
Roger Planchon, Director

With his attempt to remove Molière from the Molière-tradition by staging Dandin according to the picturesque inspiration of post-Molière realism, Planchon subjected to an examination those prejudices which have been maintained against the dramatic methods of creating an illusion. His production, therefore, did not attain to significance because of its excellent actors but because it illustrated that aesthetic truths are independent of time and need only be later manifested with the same degree of artistry as that from which they were derived. This production, by using the example of Molière (that is to say, by using a play for which one would apparently presuppose the existence of a firmly outlined, well worked out style of production), demonstrated that a play is bound less to a style of acting than to a certain degree of artistic realization. Planchon went still further: he illustrated the truth of a saying which these days is no longer held to possess much conviction, namely, the old Riccoboni-Lessing assertion that art is an imitation of nature. Planchon showed us what imitation is and in what way imitation becomes art. He reproduced in a realistic manner the visage of the world in which the comedy takes place. He complemented it by bringing more on the stage than the mere plot requires. The peasants' costumes, gait, and movements revealed their social position as well as their social consciousness. Their silent and articulated expressions (looks and laughs) and the director's arrangement of their positions on stage also revealed the play's social tensions and the responsibilities of the upper classes. . . .

Günther Rühle, in *Theater*, 1962,
yearbook of *Theater Heute*.

The Miser
Minnesota Theater Company (1963)
Douglas Campbell, Director

After all, the moon is on the verge of being attainable. With further opportunity to work its way into Mr. Campbell's approach, *The Miser* should become increasingly all of a piece. For the moment it bubbles and goes flat at intervals, only to revive suddenly with fresh sparkle.

Mr. Campbell uses the open stage imaginatively—and expects the audience to enlist its own imagination with equal eagerness. Doors and gateways are suggested by pairs of servants standing and joining outstretched arms. Chairs become walls. Passageways are where you want them, and a garden is conjured up in an instant by moving a couple of tables and dropping a handful of stage leaves.

The blithe spirit of the production is manifested at the outset by the appearance of various principals and servants—the latter all in delightful masks in the Commedia dell'Arte manner. Not a word is spoken as a drooping cloth is propped up with a pole, and pieces of furniture are arranged. The players do a graceful dance, presaging at least partly the mood of what is to come with their amusing dumb show.

Howard Taubman, *The New York Times*,
May 10, 1963.

The Miser
Minnesota Theater Company (1963)
Douglas Campbell, Director

The Miser is not only funny and charming, it's Molière. Everyone pretends to know that Molière can be funny and charming and even more than that, of course, but it's all pretending because no one ever gets to see the man's work—not in New York, and certainly not in English. The Tyrone Guthrie theater has now taken care of the matter for the citizens of Minneapolis, at least, and if a rumor should begin to radiate outward from there that Molière is playable, who can tell what might not happen.

I suppose it would have been easy enough for director Douglas Campbell simply to cover the French master's ancient farce formula with an overlay of pretty posturing and an icing of whipped-cream costumes, and then let it go at that as a graceful bow to the past. . . .

But never mind the fleet-in-full-sail costuming or the clattering busyness that Mr. Campbell has invented to keep the half-masked servants and the half-mad lovers swooping and scurrying, counter-clockwise and back, along the outer edges of the apron. . . .

What counts, if Molière is to be served at all, is the core of the comic spirit, the not entirely antic passions that stomp and fuss and then stand stock still at center stage. *The Miser* is not merely a joke. It also takes the measure of something close to a monster, and this without losing laughter or making the monster less a man. In its central role, Hume Cronyn nails the evening to the floor with the hard brass tacks of preposterous plausibility.

Walter Kerr, *New York Herald Tribune*,
May 10, 1963.

Tartuffe
Lincoln Repertory Theatre (1965)
William Ball, Director

Ball's concept of the play emphasizes its moral intensity. Instead of making Orgon the laughably gullible, pitiable victim of Tartuffe, he makes him a full and decent man whom we can respect. This Orgon is the victim of his own virtue, the virtue of trust; otherwise he is admirable, and what we feel for him is not pity or disdain but concern. Similarly, the entire family has a fine solidity of emotion among its members; these are not caricatures but persons firmly set in time and place, and all the production's high spirits and hilarity express this reality. Always we are aware of Molière's radiant moral vision, and it is this confidence in virtue that validates the play's action.

This is the inside of the play. Ball has also done a spectacular job with its outside. He does not merely keep the actors moving but uses their movements to

comment upon the words, to make a series of verbal-
visual puns that flow together as convincingly as the
writing itself. The stage picture is prettily composed
at almost every moment—something that most contemporary directors apparently forget altogether—
without jolts, without self-consciousness. It appears to
be the character's pleasure to look their best at all
times and the actors are remarkably at ease in their 17-
century clothes and manners.

Michael Smith, *The Village Voice*,

January 21, 1965.

Tartuffe
Lincoln Repertory Theatre (1965)
William Ball, Director

No doubt Mr. O'Sullivan enjoys his own
misplaced virtuosity. It isn't every day that a serious
and talented actor can make a vaudeville exercise out
of a seriously intended character. Given the terms of
the production, however, the performance tells more
about his director than it does about himself. Mr. Ball
shares with too many of his colleagues a distrust of his
material. He doesn't interpret what is there so much as
he compensates for what he thinks is missing. At times
this is not a hazard, for example in the charm he derives from moving the swaying Orgon family around
the stage as if the people formed one body, or the
brittle, delicate undertone he supplies by way of an
occasional use of harpsichord accompaniment, or, fi-

nally, the startling humor he discovers in an inanimate object, such as a broom that looks for an instant as if it could sweep on its own. Such simplicities, unfortunately, are not his common style. More typical is a taste for what can only be called the playing within plays, those bravura fantasies that engaged him so much more strongly than the harsh realities in his production two seasons ago of Pirandello's *Six Characters in Search of an Author*, and the bumbling play-acting of the Pyramus and Thisbe scene in Britten's *A Midsummer Night's Dream*, which he directed that year for the New York City Opera.

Tartuffe, of course, has no such set-piece, a tactless omission on Molière's part redressed by Mr. Ball in an ingenious fashion flattering both to him and Mr. O'Sullivan, but crippling to the play. Where Molière prepares patiently for our first view of Tartuffe by keeping him off the stage for the first two of his five acts, Mr. Ball brings him on at the very beginning, continuing to insert him regularly between scenes in a succession of dumb shows. In short, even before he opens his mouth to Molière's lines, Mr. O'Sullivan has several chances to trigger his infinite monotonies, thus ending the drama even earlier than had Mr. Ball permitted Tartuffe to enter at the moment planned by Molière. This is a *Tartuffe*, then, without dark harmonies. It is as if Bach were to be represented only by his ornaments; comedy is seen here only as an entertaining collection of imposed grace notes.

Gordon Rogoff, *Tulane Drama Review*,
Summer 1965.

The School for Wives
Phoenix Theater (1971)
Stephen Porter, Director

I go to Molière reluctantly. Two reasons. First, fascinating as old comedy often is in several ways, it's not often funny. I except most of Shakespeare and some Restoration plays, otherwise I agree with W. H. Auden that "there is hardly a line written before the middle of the eighteenth century which, on reading, can make us laugh aloud." Performance rarely helps matters.

Second, connected with the first, the comedies that still live do so by reason of their language. Translations are never good enough, in comedy. I assume that Molière, for the French-speaking, lives as Shakespeare does for me. In English, stripped of his language, Molière reduces to linear plot, in most cases, with *Commedia* characters and last-minute mechanical resolution. The clear exceptions are *Don Juan* and *Tartuffe*, whose thematic and character complexity come through in competent translation. Otherwise, with verbal richness gone, the diet is mostly thin.

Richard Wilbur, one of our best poets, has now translated several Molière comedies. French scholars call his work fine. All I hear is his English, and, reasonably deft as the verses are, the translations are just an

endless series of rhymed iambic couplets, often with
feminine endings that jingle on and on. . . .

Stanley Kauffman, The New Republic,
May 8, 1971.

The School for Wives
Phoenix Theater (1971)
Stephen Porter, Director

We never get enough classic theater in
New York. Certainly we don't get enough classic theater of the quality of the Phoenix Theater's production of Molière's *The School for Wives*. . . . It once
more shows that Molière can be funny, blithe and
totally enchanting.

A large part of the reason for what must be termed
a Molière revival in North America is the excellence
of the new verse translations by Richard Wilbur, who
has now added this *The School for Wives* to his *Misanthrope* and *Tartuffe*. The translations are deft, very
graceful and nicely unaffected. Mr. Wilbur has a sense
of humor, and although once in a while he slips into a
conversational anarchronism—the phrase "How is
your love-life?" jars in an 18th-century street—the
general effect is fresh and pure.

It is curious how masterpieces take on slightly
different aspects for different centuries. We have already seen the feminism in Ibsen's *The Doll's House*,
and now the very liberal attitude Molière took to

women is getting an airing, as well as Molière's profound belief in moderation. . . .

Arnolphe has to be pompous, arrogant, disdainful
and totally fooled. Now many a comic character is
fooled, but where Molière gives this fooling its flavor
is to have Arnolphe made into the reluctant confidant
and fellow conspirator of his rival, Horace. The result
is that Arnolphe is forever having to say one thing and
be thinking another, never being able to betray his
anger at being duped.

Clive Barnes, The New York Times,
July 17, 1971.

BIBLIOGRAPHY

PLAYS BY MOLIÈRE

La Jalousie de Barbouillé, 1645–50.
Le Médecin volant, 1645–50.
L'Étourdi, ou Les Contre-temps, 1653.
Le Dépit amoureux, 1656.
Les Précieuses ridicules, 1659.
Sganarelle, ou Le Cocu imaginaire, 1660.
Dom Garcie de Navarre, ou Le Prince jaloux, 1661.
L'École des maris, 1661.
Les Facheux, 1661.
L'École des femmes, 1662.
Critique de L'École des femmes, 1663.
L'Impromptu de Versailles, 1663.
Le mariage forcé, 1664.
La Princesse d'Élide, 1664.
Tartuffe, ou L'Imposteur, 1664–69.
Don Juan, ou Le Festin de pierre, 1665.
L'Amour médecin, 1665.
Le Misanthrope, 1664–66.

Le Médecin malgré lui, 1666.
Mélicerte, 1666.
La Pastorale comique, 1667.
Le Sicilien, ou L'Amour peintre, 1667.
Amphitryon, 1668.
Georges Dandin, ou Le Mari confondu, 1668.
L'Avare, 1668.
Monsieur de Pourceaugnac, 1669.
Les Amants magnifique, 1670.
Le Bourgeois gentilhomme, 1670.
Psyché (with Pierre Corneille and Philippe Quinault),
  1671.
Le Fourberies de Scapin, 1671.
La Comtesse d'Escarbagnas, 1671.
Les Femmes savantes, 1672.
Le Malade imaginaire, 1673.

EDITIONS IN FRENCH

Oeuvres, ed. by Vinot and C. de La Grange, 8 vols.,
  Paris, 1682.
Oeuvres, ed. by Voltaire, 6 vols. Amsterdam and Leip-
  zig, 1765.
Oeuvres complètes, ed. by René Bray, 8 vols. Paris,
  1952.
Oeuvres Complètes de Molière, annotated by Maurice
  Rat, 2 vols., Paris, 1956.

COLLECTED EDITIONS IN ENGLISH

Eight Plays by Molière, trans. and introduced by
  Morris Bishop, New York, 1957.

One-Act Comedies of Molière, trans. and introduced by Albert Bermel, Cleveland, 1964.

The Misanthrope and Other Plays, trans. by Donald M. Frame, New York, 1968.

The Miser and Other Plays, trans. by J. Wood, Baltimore, 1953.

Molière's Comedies, introduced by F. G. Green, 2 vols. New York, 1929.

The Principal Comedies of Molière, ed. and introduced by F. K. Turgeon and A. C. Gilligan, New York, 1935.

Six Prose Comedies by Molière, trans. by George Graveley, London, 1956.

Tartuffe and Other Plays, trans. by Donald M. Frame, New York, 1967.

RECOMMENDED INDIVIDUAL TRANSLATIONS

The Imaginary Invalid. In *The Genius of French Theatre*, ed. by Albert Bermel and trans. by Mildred Marmur, New York, 1961.

The Learned Ladies. In *Classical French Drama*, ed. and trans. by Wallace Fowlie, New York, 1962.

The Misanthrope and *Tartuffe.* Translated into English verse by Richard Wilbur, New York, 1965.

The School for Wives. Trans. into English verse by Richard Wilbur, New York, 1971.

SELECTED CRITICISM

Audiberti, J., *Molière dramaturge*, Paris, 1954.
Bray, René, *Molière: Homme de théâtre*, Paris, 1954.

Bulgakov, Mikhail, *The Life of Monsieur de Molière*, New York, 1970.

Chapman, Percy Addison, *The Spirit of Molière*, New York, 1965.

Charden, H., *Nouveaux documents sur les comédiens de campagne,et la vie de Molière*, 2 vols., Paris, 1968.

Chatfield-Taylor, H. C., *Molière: A Biography*, New York, 1905.

Fabre, E., *Notre Molière*, Paris, 1951.

Fernandez, Ramon, *Molière: The Man Through His Plays*, New York, 1958.

Gossman, Lionel, *Men and Masks: A Study of Molière*, Baltimore, 1963.

Lewis, D. B. Wyndham, *Molière: The Comic Mask*, New York, 1959.

Moore, W. G., *Molière: A New Criticism*, Oxford, 1962.

Teyssier, Jean Marie, *Reflexion sur le "Don Juan" de Molière*, Paris, 1970.

Turnell, Martin, *The Classical Moment: Studies of Corneille, Molière and Racine*, New York, 1946.

INDEX

34
86-98
21